MINOR
MONUMENTS

For Nana & John Joe

MINOR
MONUMENTS
essays
IAN MALENEY

TRAMPPRESS

First published 2019 by Tramp Press
www.tramppress.com

'And the Wind It Tremendously Blew'
appeared in *Winter Papers* (Volume 3)
'Shelter' appeared in *The Dublin Review* (Issue 70)
An extract from an early version of 'Pneumonia'
appeared in the *Wire* magazine (Issue 304)

A CIP record for this title is available
from The British Library.

1 3 5 7 9 10 8 6 4 2

ISBN 978–1–9164342–0–2

Tramp Press gratefully acknowledges the
support of the Arts Council, Ireland.

Thank you for supporting independent publishing.

Set in 11 pt on 17 pt Galliard by Marsha Swan.
Printed by Clays, London.

contents

My father's father, his father's father, his —
Shadows like winds.
—Wallace Stevens, 'The Irish Cliffs of Moher'

and the wind it
tremendously blew

The first time Niamh came with me to my parents' farm, I took her to the bog. It's not much of a destination, but it's about the only place you can go if you want to get out of the house. We followed the road down by my grandparents' place, which is next door to ours, and around the back of the cattle-sheds. At the end of our fields there's a shaded lane that takes you through to where the bog begins. The lane forks at the end and becomes two grass-covered paths that go deeper into the bog.

We hung a right towards the elevated, heather-covered bank where my grandparents used to save their turf. Getting to the high bank means wading through some tall, stiff grass growing from very wet ground. Even in summer it can be a messy business. Neither of us were adequately dressed, but we got as far as the bottom of the bank and stood for a while next to a sheer six-foot face of deep brown peat. Niamh took a photo of me there with her phone. I had my hands in the pockets of my hoodie and I looked back over my shoulder towards her, wind-blown, my face balled up in a squint. Upon uploading it to Facebook, she added the caption,

> *Out here in Jutland*
> *In the old man-killing parishes*
> *I will feel lost*
> *Unhappy and at home.*

—

The previous summer we had visited the Douglas Hyde Gallery in Dublin. In the small secondary exhibition space, there was an installation of Richard Skelton's *Landings* project. *Landings* consists of a book and some record-ings: multiple copies of the book were attached to a long table, and each was matched with a pair of headphones. I listened to slow waves of violin and concertina as the words on the pages overflowed the edges of form. What started out as a fragmentary diary became a torrent of words arrayed in grids or lists. Sometimes a remnant of a line would sit alone in the middle of the page. Others were black with accumulations of old words, forgotten words, everyday words. The names for places were the most interesting. Anglezarke and Rivington, Old Rachel's and Hordern Stoops: the complete foreignness of the language was amazing to me.

The heavy bell of time sounded in *Landings'* fascination with weathering, with decay, and with the ineluctable loss of words, homes, ways of life. I read as figures and dates became covered in moss, walls collapsed, archives petered out and the wind blew right through. In the book's darkest moments, sense faded from the world and there was nothing left but the evidence, everywhere apparent, of its disappearance.

I got a glimpse of the person behind these visions: a man, not yet old, who had lost his young wife to an early death. 1975–2004. 'I wanted to tell you about the river,' he writes. *Landings*, it is soon clear, is a record of living with the kind of loss which forever tips the scales of life. Grieving, enduring. I won't say moving on.

Retreating to the depopulated Lancashire moors, Skelton found himself burying instruments in the ground. He found himself playing them, the strings and his hands both covered in dirt. He found himself playing along with the wind and the rivers, offering up notes to the elements of air, soil, water. 'I want to make some kind of gesture,' he writes. 'An offering. A mark of passing.' Skelton wandered the moor, the fields, the woodlands, the riverbanks – 'constantly roaming, never dwelling' – adrift in this circumscribed territory where he was living without ever being quite at home.

While time passed incessantly in the book, the music seemed oddly still. It lingered. It drew single moments out into great durations, droning, holding, repeating. It was as if only sound, only song, could calm the destabilising enormity of the past and arrest that quivering shadow of grief. 'Whilst I dwelt within that wooded chamber, listening to those brief glimmers of song, I forgot about her, the river, and its promise.'

I was instantly captivated by *Landings*, and I returned to the gallery repeatedly during its exhibition. There was something in its openness, its vulnerability, its sense of being unfinished and ongoing, which seemed to invite a response from me. There was a level of abstraction which was welcoming, even comforting. The feeling was similar to that of my first exposure to Heaney's poems, which suggested that the kind of place I came from could be the stuff of poetry and not just a blank and backward wilderness from which to escape. Skelton's art – in words, but more directly in the sounds which surrounded them – was rarely possessed of Heaney's poise, but that was all the better. The roughness of its construction was more immediate and more attainable. I felt as if I could respond in kind. I started walking the bog.

—

Sometime between *Landings* and Niamh's first visit to the bog, we went to see *Silence*, a film by Pat Collins. It's rare you find a piece of work that seems to have been made with you in mind, but when I first saw *Silence* I felt as if it had been created purely for my benefit.

The film's central character is Eoghan, a sound recordist who is returning to Ireland after fifteen years away. Eoghan's task is to record silence – to record spaces which are empty of human interference, environments free of 'unnatural' interruption. In the first place where Eoghan stays overnight, a barman tells him a story about an island off the coast of Scotland, uninhabited for fifty years, where the starlings still make the sound of the mowing machines the islanders used in the 1950s. 'They passed it down from generation to generation of starling.' He looks at Eoghan – 'Would that be the kind of story you're …?' When Eoghan says that it's not stories but quietness he's after, the barman looks puzzled, and a little smile crosses his face as he flips over his newspaper. 'You'd want to be careful of that,' he says. 'Too much quietness would drive a fella mad.'

When Eoghan stands in the silence of Mullaghmore, that great limestone hill in the Burren, a thin voice gently warped by magnetic tape drifts across on the wind. This faint song is enough to disturb our protagonist. You don't want to be hearing voices on the wind. The song seems to originate in a ruined house which sometimes flickers into view like a trick of the light. The song comes from the same space, but not the same time. They glide past each other, an uncanny misalignment.

Eoghan carries the past around with him, much as Skelton does in *Landings*. But where music calms Skelton's ghosts, Eoghan's appear in the form of a song. For Skelton, the escape into sound takes him away from language, away from memories almost too painful to bear. It only lasts a few moments, but that respite is enough to suggest there is yet a way to live, that there is a space outside of grief.

Eoghan would appear to be moving in the opposite direction. He is making his way back to his childhood home on Tory Island, drawn by a melody which has taken root in him, a fragment of a tape he made when he was a child. The sound of his parents and their neighbours in their old house, talking, singing. The wind howling outside. A mourning he has tried to outrun. The closer he gets to the silence he's come to find, the more powerful this old voice becomes – it is the sound of a past life, a half-forgotten language, a decimated people.

—

The bog is a quiet place. No matter how often I go there, no matter how closely I listen, it remains a quiet place. There are three primary sounds: the wind in the scattered trees, the birds, and the remote sounds which are not of the bog but which are audible there all the same; chainsaws, lawnmowers, tractors – engines beyond the horizon. These elements combine in different measures on different days. A windless day leaves the far-off hums exposed and sharpens the hollow bark of a dog on a distant farm. The birds come alive in the early evening and their pinprick calls are soft and charming. On a stormy day there is nothing but wind; a dull blast obliterating all else as it makes its way across the plain.

I have stood in all kinds of weather out on the high bank with my recorder aloft. Standing up there once, I could hear a very faint drone, a sound I thought might be a train, or even motorway traffic on the far side of the Shannon. Something miles and miles away. Rooted like a tree as the minutes crawled past, I closed my eyes and tried in vain to make sense of this vague shadow of a sound. Then I looked up. A gigantic swarm of midges were forming a dark, humming cloud a foot above my head. My legs took action before my head had time to think and I ran wildly towards home, plunging through the chest-high grass. Breathless at the edge of the bog, my vision of myself as an intrepid field recordist in tatters, I began to laugh at my instinct for flight.

—

I think my favourite part of *Silence* comes when Eoghan meets Michael Harding, the writer and actor. Harding comes striding through a field of pale yellow grass – 'How're ya doing? Windy day!' Eoghan explains that he's recording areas free of man-made sound. 'But sure you're here,' Harding says. 'I'm here,' Eoghan replies, 'but I'm keeping quiet.'

Together they drive back to Harding's house. Harding asks Eoghan what the Irish word for silence would be. Eoghan suggests *ciuineas*, which means calm or relief, and *suaimhneas*, which means rest. '*Suaimhneas siorrai do annamh*,' is the Irish version of the funeral prayer, 'Eternal rest grant unto them O Lord,' and a common inscription on the gravestones of Tory Island.

Harding has another suggestion: '*Bí i do thost.*'

'*Cad é sin i mBéarla?*' he asks, '*Tost?*'

Eoghan has no answer – there is no direct translation into English. *Tost*, Eoghan explains, is the 'gap between noise'.

'You have to have noise to get *tost*,' he says. '*Tost* is in between.'

Tost is a silence that implies its own interruption, a silence which makes sense of that which surrounds it. Silence, *tost* suggests, does not happen solely in the present – it retains an awareness of what has come before and what is yet to come.

—

In my early days of recording the bog, I would just leave my recorder atop a fencepost and walk away for an hour or so. At first I found the disconnection between what I heard and what the recorder heard to be exciting. I didn't know what I would find when I played the file back at home. As time went on, the disconnection began to grate. I wasn't recording the place for some objective posterity. I wasn't a scientist tracking the wildlife or weather patterns. What was I recording for if not to remind myself of what it is like for a particular person to be there, in a particular place at a particular time? Being there, listening – this is my gesture, my offering, my mark of passing. Walking away from the recorder I lost that possibility and, in a way, I gave up the responsibility of it. Instead of coming to listen more closely to every moment, using the recorder as a means to heighten the senses, I passed off the task of listening to it. I would wander around while it worked on my behalf. I might as well never have been there at all.

I have accumulated hours and hours of recorded emptiness. Some days have been experiments; dropping microphones into the drains and listening as the water sludges past the silicone, or duct-taping them to trees in a downpour, hearing the drops ring against the bark. Sometimes I'm drawn to an event, like when someone burned a great stack of recently felled trees. The fire smouldered for days while the smoke drifted all across the bog. But drama like that is rare. Most often, I'm just walking without aim or destination.

The landscape of the walker is always a subjective and temporal experience, something which must be under-gone, something in which I immerse or submerge myself. Walking is like listening in this respect. It has no end. This is why I make recordings, and I think why Eoghan holds a microphone instead of a camera. I think it explains, too, why there are no photographs in *Landings*.

When I'm out walking and recording, I'm not capturing the environment in any kind of objective way. I'm just being swept along with it until I press stop. What I've recorded is not so much an accurate replication of the time spent listening as it is a personal reminder that the time was spent at all. The material result is rarely my concern; what matters is the closeness to the process, how it seems to saturate my experience, my perception. When the small red light is on, I hold my breath and feel every breeze, every raindrop, and every insect against my skin. When I play the files back later, they are like flash cards helping me to remember a particular experience of sound and place. I play them over and over. I want to internalise that experience, to hold it safe within me, to feel no distance from it at all.

—

After dinner in Harding's house, the two men begin to talk. The room is half-lit, the night grown dark. Harding is asking after Eoghan's family.

– You're an only child?

– I am, aye.

– Parents?

Eoghan does not reply. A silence falls. Harding says this is his mother's house. That when he is there, he can

experience a kind of silence. He means it in a metaphys-
ical sense. A quietness of the mind. The camera lingers
on Eoghan as Harding talks to him from off-screen. He
seems to be retreating into himself. He says very little.
Eventually Harding breaks the mood.

– Anyway, we'll have a song please. Do you know 'The
Rocks of Bawn'? A Cavan song.

– I heard it alright. My grandfather sang it. I never
learned it.

—

Niamh and I returned to the bog some years after that first
visit, to record sounds for a project she was working on.
She wanted to capture the squelching and burbling of the
sodden ground. I jumped in and out of liquid earth, lost
a wellington, made all sorts of noises. On our way home,
we walked through my grandparents' back yard where my
grandmother was filling buckets of turf. We stopped to
chat with Nana for a while, and my grandfather came out
to join us.

John Joe wasn't particularly mobile at this stage, and I
remember how long it took him to cross the narrow strip
of concrete to where we were standing. He was nearly
bent double over his walking stick. 'He won't even know
who you are until he comes over near you now, honestly,'
Nana said as he shuffled towards us. She warned Niamh
that he would repeatedly ask her the same questions.

'Do you know this fella, John Joe?' she said.

'Ah, I'd know now if I could get time to look at him,' came the reply. 'Oh Lord, I know you well but I just can't put a name on you.'

Nana explained to him that I was his grandson, that I was from just up the garden. You could tell he was better at bluffing than he was at remembering. When he found out Niamh lived in Dublin, he sang a little bit of 'Molly Malone' for her. Always a charmer, he took her hand and said she was a lovely girl, a lovely, lovely girl. 'Don't squeeze the hand off her now, you were very fond of them,' Nana said. 'I'm not!' he protested, laughing. 'That's what has me in trouble now with you.'

Nana pushed him again to remember who I was. 'We reared him,' she said. 'Well,' he replied, 'we dragged him up.' We talked a little about my brothers, the cattle my father had recently bought, the way the weeks were passing quicker than ever. As ever, Nana couldn't get over how it was October already, the year nearly gone. John Joe piped up. 'It's like the woman said one time when she pegged the clock out through the window – time flies.' The Alzheimer's is a curse, as Nana would say, but it's easier if you've got a sense of humour.

When we left, they walked together towards the back door of the house, bickering playfully about tea-time and slices of currant bread. I can only remember all this because Niamh had accidentally left the recorder running. It had been working the entire time, recording the conversation from a pocket of her backpack. She cut this section out for me, and I have it still. It's only three years ago, but it feels like so much longer. As the clip ends, their voices are fading away, becoming quieter and quieter still.

—

Mourning, Fanny Howe writes, teaches us to love without an object. I feel like listening teaches us the same thing.

—

During the final two or three years of his life, I made many surreptitious recordings of John Joe as he sat by the fire in their kitchen. He was in the process of forgetting almost everything he'd ever known. He was fading out of the world, and I began to grieve long before the death was final. I wanted to record whatever it was he might say before it was too late. Not because what he had to say was particularly significant or even memorable, but because no one would ever say anything like it again.

It occurred to me that, while there would be many pictures of him from throughout his life, there would be very few recordings of his voice. I find it much harder to recall a voice I haven't heard in years than a face I haven't seen. Roland Barthes wrote in the opening pages of his *Mourning Diary* that his mother's voice, 'the very texture of memory', had gone silent in his mind. He called it a 'local-ised deafness'.

The recordings I made of John Joe are not good: I made them mostly on my phone, because I didn't want anyone to know I was making them. I left the phone down wherever, paid it no heed. The results are quiet and hiss-filled but I think no less eloquent or compelling for that. The earlier recordings are filled with chat. Nearer the end, voices emerge only intermittently from the encroaching silence of the kitchen. He was losing his voice along with his memories. The words barely make it out of his throat.

Regardless of their fidelity, the recordings suggest a depth, a duration, and a movement to what photographs of him have frozen flat and static. A person's face is not exactly still, but it is less dynamic and, in a way, less personal than their voice. A photograph of a person who has since died does not make them seem alive again, but a recording of their voice can be enough to recall them to the room, to make their presence felt. My favourite record-ings are those where John Joe sings along with the radio. He sang old songs, the songs all old people know. He sang 'Carrickfergus', he sang 'Eileen McMahon', he sang 'I'll Be Your Sweetheart'. He sang songs they'd later play at his funeral, songs like 'The Rocks of Bawn'. He had forgotten most of everything, but scraps of melody remained. They were hidden in that part of the brain where treasures are kept, alongside the name of his wife, Kathleen.

—

When I started walking the bog, I thought I had to listen for something particular. I thought I would hear what others hadn't heard, that I would go out there in order to capture something surprising, something novel. I was waiting for something significant to appear to me through the silence. I thought I was going to make something of all this, that my superior artistic impulses would rescue from obscurity something that everyone else had missed. I thought my work would prove, once and for all, the value of this place for which no one else seemed to care. It took quite a lot of exposure to the bog's particular hush before I realised that, for all my sincere concentration, I was missing the point.

Silence, the kind of silence that you get in the bog, is not the absence of sound. It's a lower order of sound, an experience of extremely diminished sound. The 'basement of listening', David Toop calls it – a place to which you descend. It is the kind of quiet which allows thoughts to bubble up inside you. When almost all sound is taken away, the sounds that remain take on a greater definition and a greater weight. What before was indistinct can become clear as day; what was obscured or concealed can come finally to our attention.

Most of all, silence insists on sound. It gives us the possibility of sound, of music, of understanding. It is silence that makes language intelligible. Without it, all our words would just run together. If the balance between sound and silence is off, communication quickly becomes impossible.

Silence is the pause between notes that gives us rhythm, patterns, sense. Debussy said that silence was perhaps the only way of making the emotion of a phrase gain its true weight. Silence is not just a passive experience, but an operative agent in our recognition of the world. Everything comes out of it, lives alongside it, is perforated by it, and eventually vanishes back into it.

Sound and silence are two sides of the same coin, a breeze blowing at different strengths. We cannot know in advance the voices that might be heard when the wind is low. Walking the bog, I am learning to listen to that wind, however it blows.

—

Just before he arrives back on Tory, Eoghan tells a story recollected from his childhood. Speaking now in Irish, he recalls sitting at home at night with his mother, listening on a CB radio to his father and his fellow island fishermen as they work out in the ocean beyond Tory, talking to each other across the waves. 'And some nights when they were in good form and the night was calm, you'd hear a fragment of a song coming over the radio,' he says. 'They'd sing songs to each other from one boat to the next, the sound travelling over the waves. Sometimes it was so faint, almost not there, as if you were imagining it.'

Listening takes us beyond the horizon of sight. I can imagine the fishermen, out there in the dark Atlantic, working to make a life for themselves and their loved ones back on land. The sound of their voices coming faintly through the night air is proof of survival. The songs they sing are proof of a particular life, and their stories float like mist through the atmosphere. For the young boy sitting in the dark at home, listening to these songs, these disembodied voices must have had some power. Were the words important, or was it just sound itself that was hoped for? On stormy nights, they would listen carefully for any sound over the radio. 'There would be no songs then.' It's hard to imagine a more vivid absence than the longed-for sound of a familiar voice in the night; transient, immaterial, unimaginably important. A frail speck atop the ocean spray, the weight of the world resting upon it.

below

When we are lost in darkness and see a distant glimmer of light, who does not dream of a thatched cottage or, to go more deeply still into legend, of a hermit's hut?

—Gaston Bachelard, *The Poetics of Space*

I can't say when the foundations of my grandparents' house were laid. Some ancestor of mine has lived without distinction or fame on that patch of heavy, unproductive land for at least two hundred years. When Richard Griffith conducted his Primary Valuation – the first full-scale assessment of property in Ireland – in the years immediately after the Famine, my family was already there, probably surviving hand-to-mouth in bog-side hovels. Like everyone else in the area, they were paying rent to the Rev. James Alexander of the local Protestant church. Their houses cost them one pound and five shillings annually, and land to farm was extra.

Two homes were recorded there during the census of 1911: one where the house still stands today, the other possibly where the cattle sheds are. By the time John Joe was born in 1933, the main house was thatched. Forty years later, the thatch was removed and the house was crowned with its current slate roof.

It is a house that was made by adding one room onto another until there were enough rooms. Outside, it boasts pebbledash walls, painted white, with a trim of something warmer along the bottom and around the windows. White gutters, white window frames, a white front door. Inside, the house is compact – boxy rooms, narrow halls, all centred on the kitchen and the fireplace. Fifty years ago, part of the kitchen was a bedroom. When Nana first moved in, my great-grandfather slept there. Though I never met him, I'm fairly sure he also had some form of dementia. Nana told me that he once threw a knife at her from across the kitchen; it stuck in the wooden door of the cupboard beside her head, quivering. He was found dead out behind the cattle sheds in March of 1972.

All the living is done in the kitchen. It is a long, rectangular room, split in two. The smaller section – where the bedroom used to be – contains the sink, the fridge, a dresser, and the cupboards where the cups and plates are kept. There are two countertops now where the old dividing wall used to be, with the gap between them opening out onto the rest of the room. The kettle is next the sink, and between it and the television there is a clear plastic box filled with colourful medication.

The larger part of the kitchen is arranged around the fireplace. For many years there was a white tin range against the wall, with a metal shelf above it for drying clothes. When John Joe came in from work, he would lean his arms against the shelf and allow his then-giant frame to soak up the heat from below. Today there is a thick, black iron stove there, with four minuscule legs and a glass door. It is much more beautiful, and warmer too. Every day starts with the lighting of the fire, and it burns until after everyone has gone to sleep. Nana cleans the glass every morning, so that the flames are clearly visible.

Sunlight pours into the kitchen through the square box-window set into the front of the house. At certain times in spring and autumn, when the days are just the right length, the window catches the setting sun for a few moments before it disappears. The light is weak, but it is enough to make the room glow for a while before the lights are turned on. The shadows grow long on the pale linoleum floor, the fire burns muted and warm, and there is an incredible sense of stillness. It's a room where you can really feel the night falling. There's a clock above the table on the opposite wall, and beside that, the ruby glimmer of the sacred heart.

—

My grandparents' house was the first place outside our home that my two brothers and I had licence to explore. There is only a hundred yards between the houses, but their place felt like a different country to us as children.

It was close enough to home for it to be safe, but still distant enough to encourage adventure and imagination. Unlike home, we had no responsibilities there, no chores or duties, and no space designated as our own. We were less supervised there, and we had permission to roam, to pull things apart, to construct whatever we desired. Mostly, we desired huts.

Our most basic huts were hollowed-out stretches of roadside ditch, barely wide enough to slip our tiny bodies through. We had one such hut on the hill that rises around Nana's house. The bushes on the hill were little more than tangles of briars. Clearing out the middle of this almighty knot meant getting thorns lodged in your skin, and coming home with scratches all down your arms and face. We probably used a hacksaw borrowed from my grandfather's shed, and a wire-cutters too. At one point – I'm sure of it – we had a scythe. We cut and chopped a tunnel through the bushes, sawing off branches and casting them behind us. The floor of the hut was bare earth, with a few old pillows scattered across it. A rug was co-opted at one stage, just thin and long enough to fit. The walls were the rough edges of the bushes, and they folded over us to create a thick roof that wasn't quite rain-proof. The whole effect was that of a cave, which widened a little at its deepest point, and we spent most of one summer in there.

I can't remember now how it smelled or how it felt to touch; it exists only as a memory of rough shapes and abstract sensation. I do know it was warm, most of the

time, and lit just enough by the strong summer sun. I
suppose it could fit about half a dozen children, none
more than ten years old. Mostly it was me and my brothers.
There would be our two cousins from up the road, and the
neighbour's kids too. There weren't many houses around,
and fewer again with children, so we were a small group,
all near enough the same age. I was the oldest, except for
a few weeks a year when my American cousin, ten months
my senior, would visit. With just one exception, we were
all boys. We played card games and board games. We
complained about not being allowed to watch television.
We fought and argued and fell out. We talked about plans
for other, better huts most of all; we were always moving
onto the next thing. It doesn't really matter what we did
or said in the hut – it was never meant to be remembered.

What I do remember is that feeling of carving out
a space of our own, away from the eyes and ears of our
parents. Transgression was latent in the arrangement, and
nothing had to actually *occur* for it to seem illicit. Just being
in a place where they couldn't quite control us, where
they wouldn't know exactly what happened, was enough
of a thrill to make it worthwhile. The nascent realisation
that our lives were our own prompted us to build the
huts, and in them we could explore our emerging iden-
tities, try out new words or poses, say and do things that
would be embarrassing or forbidden in the house just a
few yards away.

—

Nana complains often that houses are not as open as they used to be. She had an expectation, in her younger days, that she could knock on any door and be invited in for tea. Anyone who showed up at her door would have received the same courtesy. In part, this is down to her growing older, not knowing the people who live around her so well. But it's also due to the changing ways that people work, the greater distances they travel every day, and the decreasing likelihood that the house would contain a permanent homemaker.

When Nana was younger, most of the people she knew followed similar schedules throughout the day, and across the year. When a certain task on the farm needed extra hands, she would end up feeding everyone that came to help. When they became the first in the area to have their own television, half the parish would show up on Sunday afternoons to watch football and hurling, and Nana would spend her time bringing them tea, biscuits, and cake. In the evenings, friends and family would come rambling for drinks and chat. My grandparents and their friends worked together in fields, ate together in each others' kitchens, and drank together in the same pubs. Their lives were far more intertwined and co-dependent even than my parents' generation.

The most formal gatherings were station masses, held by each house in turn. Our corner of the parish had a strictly regulated circuit which brought the priest to a different house every six months. One mass in spring, the next in autumn. When I was young, the circuit took about six years to loop back around to the start. That circuit isn't operational any more, and I'm not sure that anyone really takes a station mass now. Though I found them boring as a child, particularly if I had to serve at them, I think now there was something positive about the ritual of the station, the way the private space of the home was opened up in a manner both formal and welcoming. Once you got the mass out of the way, it really wasn't that bad. It is a pity that nothing more secular has replaced it; the occasion made homes, and the people who lived in them, much more approachable – less walled off, less like castles.

The gatherings I remember best were family occasions. My grandparents' house was perfect for these because it was a place where everyone felt equally comfortable, equally at home. It would have been much more difficult, particularly in more recent years, to convince Nana and John Joe to come even as far as our house at the other end of the garden. They were happy in their own place, with their family around them. Everyone else had the freedom to come and go as they wished. I sometimes think of the image of their house at night, seen from ours, with the porch light on, a yellow glow in the kitchen window, and half a dozen cars sleeping outside. The last stop on a narrow road to nowhere, the last house before the wastes of the bog. Birthdays, Christmases, anniversaries, engagements, flying visits, fond farewells, births, deaths; all were marked by the coming together of people in that house, the last light in the dark.

I don't think just any house can achieve this. It's a function of the people who live there, not a by-product of design or architectural intent. The house, even now, has a lived-in quality that encourages more life to pass through, and to linger. It isn't comfort exactly that creates this, it is more like an accumulation of energy over time – a human energy which has sprung from this place and periodically returns. Maybe it never truly left. I think of it like lines leading outward from this centre, lines that can always be followed back to their source. People gather there and they bring that energy with them; a restorative energy in some ways, but also a force of potential. I am a product of that energy, and its conduit also.

The gaps between these gatherings invite reflection on how each differs from the last. They are occasions to think, briefly and not unhappily, about the passing of time, about how all these tall young men crowding the kitchen were, not so long ago, crawling around on that floor and being bathed in that sink. You might find yourself thinking about marriages that have fallen apart, or the ones that lasted; friendships half-forgotten, or the memory of those who have died. I think it is a house where the past lives as a peaceful tenant of the present. My grandparents' house makes change and loss seem bearable because you know these walls will remember, whenever people gather here.

—

Our hut-building didn't stop when we were teenagers, but it changed in character. My brother and I began to play music – loud music. Soon after he bought his first drum-kit, we took over one of the smaller cattle sheds at the back of my grandparents' house. It really was a cattle shed: concrete floor, bare block walls, tin roof, two sliding metal doors, and a pen for sick or calving animals. No heat, a single naked lightbulb. When my dad eventually agreed to let us have the place, he rewired the shed to give us plug sockets. A little later, he built a dividing wall to cut the shed in half and permanently separate us from the cattle. We foraged for scraps of old carpet to cover the floor, and secured a long, ratty couch that a neighbour was throwing out. John Joe came across a filing cabinet somewhere and brought it home for us. We covered one of the walls with pale green paint we'd found on a neglected shelf elsewhere in the sheds. On this base we painted our names in bright orange, with thick black outlines, and dated it. Those names are still there.

That shed was our last and most perfect hut. It was a place we could go to close the door, to make noise and dream. It was a hideaway from the world that allowed us to imagine different lives, to think up sounds and words and ideas without anyone looking over our shoulders. I can remember some of my earliest moments of real teenage angst in there – sitting in the dark with interminable feedback rising from a dirt-cheap electric guitar, half-coherent sentences filling up notebooks at a prodigious pace. I was not a happy teenager: I was stubborn, and nervous, and I was jealous of my brother because he had friends to play music with, and I did not. I hovered around the shed when he and his friends were there, acting like I was doing them a favour when really it was the other way around. He was, and is, a talented drummer, while I have never had an aptitude for instruments. We had very different tastes in music, and we fought all the time, but we also discovered ways for us to be around each other; ways for both of us to get something useful out of working together.

The shed at the back of my grandparents' house was not just a temporary lab for personal experimentation, but a testing ground for the ideas we would take with us when we outgrew it. What we did there, the rules we made for ourselves, the ideas we came up with – gradually, they became things we wanted to keep.

—

All of our huts existed in the orbit of my grandmother's house, not our own. I think now that the incredible durability of the place, the sense that it had been there for the longest time, and would be there for a considerable time yet, allowed us, even as children, to imprint ourselves upon it without worry or consequence. My grandparents and their home made us feel like we would be supported. We couldn't break what was already there, and it was solid enough to let us build on top of it. As soon as we went inside at night, the sheds, the yard, and the fields would revert to normality, unflustered by our designs. They would all be ready again tomorrow.

An ideal hut is a place that allows us to act as if nothing has ever happened before. As if we were living at the dawn of time. It's a form of primitivism that affords us the privilege of reassembling the world as we wish it to be. In a hut, we can create and enforce our own rules on virgin territory. Huts are temporary and private – what happens in one seems to be forgotten as soon as it is broken up, as it must eventually be. A hut can never last, nor can the transgressions, however mild, that might have happened within. The sin disappears with the structure. It is not just forgotten; it is as if it never happened at all. For me, huts are the physical mirrors of childhood summers.

By contrast, an ideal house is a place to live in peace with everything that has already happened. It's a structure to help us bear the weight of all that is past. I dream of my grandparents' house now because it is the strongest shelter I have experienced against time's many erosions. Though it is small, it has accommodated so much. Lives come and go there, same as anywhere else, but it's like everything given to that house has been preserved, or everything vital at least. It has withstood so much change, and the marks of those who have inhabited it are engraved in its walls.

It is simple, but it is not primitive – if a house could be said to be wise, you could call it wise.

My grandparents' house is not an escape, or not just that. Rather, it gives us back to life. Its routines and procedures are resolute, despite our comings and goings; they bend, but they do not break. Its structures, its habits, have given me a foundation for thinking about how I act in the world, and the strength to think I can survive what comes my way. And still, because it is not the place where I slept each night and woke each morning, because there is no part of it to which I could lay claim, it retains its difference, its distance. I can inhabit it imaginatively, without the duties and responsibilities of a place I would call my own. It has a history that precedes me, and a symbolic register that transcends me. It remains always something other than property.

season of migration

Each sound in itself, he said. Each passing moment in itself.
—Gabriel Josipovici, *Infinity: The Story of a Moment*

John Joe was in the first bed on the right as I entered the ward. Two nurses were holding him down by his arms and he was staring at them with wild, terrified eyes. He clearly had no idea where he was, who these people were, or what he was doing there. They kept trying to talk him down, telling him to relax, telling him to take it easy. His head swivelled as he shouted back at them. He was swamped by the bed, covered in white sheets, thin wisps of hair floating above his pale, frantic head. Even in that state, there was a strength in him that took the nurses by surprise. His arms were long and thin, but they could still exert some force; each nurse needed both hands to keep his fists from swinging.

My grandfather had that morning been admitted to Tallaght hospital in Dublin for a kidney operation. The procedure had gone to plan, but he had woken up very confused and agitated after his anaesthetic wore off. My parents were driving up to stay with him for the evening, but they were still two hours away. Living much closer to the hospital, I was asked to get there first, in the hope that I could calm him down a little. They thought a familiar face would do some good.

I have always hated hospitals, and I still feel deeply uncomfortable when I find myself in one for any reason at all. I am more unnerved by the firm professionalism and the stoic faces than the intimacy of sickness and death. I have never been more than a visitor in a hospital as an adult, so I'm always on the periphery of whatever situation has brought me there. I'm never the one the doctors approach, never the one who takes the phone calls, the one who arranges the food, the card, the flowers, or the one who brings a spare cardigan from the wardrobe at home. I have always been an observer by the hospital bed, standing mutely with my brothers as someone else does the talking and the organising. No matter my level of interest or empathy, I have to try hard not to look bored. When it comes to hospitals, I have retained the attitude and demeanour of a child.

That afternoon I was going to be, even if only temporarily, the first point of contact for the doctors and nurses. I didn't really know what was going on, but I would have to try to answer questions, try to be the necessary liaison between John Joe and the hospital staff. My actions

– asking for my grandfather's ward at reception, navi-
gating the featureless corridors and elevators, talking
to the nurses on his floor – were guided more by what
I'd seen people do on television than any personal intuition or experience. I tried to think of myself as an actor.
I felt I could follow the script and people would point me
in the right direction. I would just keep trying to hit my
cues, make sure I was facing the right way, keep moving
through the scene.

—

I barely slept that summer. Through the bars that covered
my bedroom window in Dublin, I would watch the sun
come up most mornings. Once it became bright, I would
sleep for two or three hours before getting up again.
I began to see the dawn hours as the most beautiful, as
those most suffused with potential. Through the night I
would listen out for the sounds of the church bells ringing
on the hours. With my window open to the June night,
I counted the tolls, seeing in my mind the spires from
which each had come. I was surrounded by churches then,
living in the oldest part of Dublin. I could see two from
the window, and there must have been half a dozen more
within earshot, each as distinct in the dark as they were in
daylight. The bells were travelling past me, signals in some
relay, and they were deep and clear as they spread, uninterrupted, out across the city.

I balanced my portable recorder on the sill inside the window, which was open just a crack, hoping to capture something of the atmosphere. I failed every time. Sometimes sound is essentially a function of the light, inseparable from the colour of the air it passes through. The bells permeated a deep, watery blue with a texture like rough paper. Without that light, the sounds became thin and distant, lacking completely the startling sense of proximity they possessed in real time. Sitting on my bed, lit only by the blue glow from the window, it felt like I was draped in that sound, shrouded in that light.

During the day, I was drawn repeatedly to the fountain in the small park beside the cathedral next my house. I would stand there with my recorder and my headphones, pointing the microphone this way and that, balancing the water with the birds calling out as they dropped from the trees to the rubbish bins, the sound of the children in the playground, the milling tourists. The fountain was not much to look at, but its affable trickle mingled peacefully with the lives passing round. It stood in the centre of the park, as distant from the roaring traffic as could be. Walking in from the gate, the fountain would gradually replace the cars and buses as the dominant sound, becoming clearer with every step. I find it is much more difficult to linger in urban places than the relative emptiness of the country-side, but the fountain seemed to invite a slow approach and a moment of calm. I would sit there for an hour or more, listening, sometimes reading, often just watching people as they passed.

At night, sitting upright on the bed by my window, I would play back my recordings of the fountain. I let them join with the sounds of the night, with the sounds of the bells. In those capacious dawn hours, I would sit with my laptop and mix my recordings from day and night into minute sounds; loops that I listened to while falling asleep, and never saved.

—

I remember John Joe kicking back the sheets of the hospital bed, the legs of his pyjama bottoms riding up and exposing the unblemished skin of his shins and calves. I don't think I'd ever seen his naked legs before, and I was really shocked by how smooth and lean they were. They were almost the legs of a child. His worn face and his scorched hands – the only skin of his with which I was then familiar – bore the marks of a lifetime's hard work. His calves were different – they were innocent, protected. I didn't know what to make of them.

If I swing my legs out from under the duvet in the morning, and stay a moment sitting on the edge of the bed, looking down, I now think of his legs in that hospital bed, forcing themselves out from beneath the sheets. The recognition is immediate, the similarity uncanny. Even the bend of the knee outlined against the tartan pyjama pattern is the same, the sad curve of the foot poking out the bottom comparably abject. Once I noticed it, I couldn't stop. Sometimes I find myself just sitting there, staring at my own feet and thinking of his.

—

Joan Didion once wrote that it is easy to see the beginning of things, and harder to know the end. From this remove, it seems to me as if that summer became both at once – a period of months when two distinct velocities overlapped and cancelled each other out. I was caught between them, unable to take meaningful steps in any direction. I passed that summer without thinking; I did whatever came easiest, whatever could be done without having to make a serious decision. I went along with everything and everyone and for a while there it seemed like it was working out.

It was my first summer out of college, a moment I had been anticipating for some time. I'd spent the previous three years in the frustrating half-way house of a suburban campus, commuting between there, the country, and the city, never feeling properly at home anywhere. My days and weeks were defined by the many fallow hours I spent on buses – not sleeping, but not quite awake either. Now, my responsibilities to my parents regarding my education had been seen through and I was free to make my own way. I embraced that freedom and immediately began excising my rural upbringing, ploughing guiltlessly into what I thought of as a world of cultured urban possibility.

I set about worming my way into the artistic milieu I had longed to experience as a teenager in the countryside, back when I'd hoarded whatever diluted artefacts of the creative life I could, after they'd filtered down to the middle of nowhere. Thanks to a combination of accident, desperation, and a lack of better ideas, I found myself writing about music to make my rent. Historically speaking, this has never been a healthy or profitable occupation, and it remained so when I embarked upon it. At the start of the summer I moved in with my friend Dave, who was a few years older than me, and made decent money running student nights around town. Dave was tall, handsome and very charming – a real people person, genuinely interested in what you were doing, and always thinking of ways to do exciting work of his own. He was from the country too, and had left behind a sensible career in the construction industry to spend nights in loud, glittery nightclubs. We worked together a lot – DJing, recording bands, making plans. Dave could talk to anyone, and I was happy to tag along. I felt like I could learn a lot from him.

Living with Dave was fun, but I wasn't making enough money. Every month I would lie and tell our landlady, a middle-aged woman, indistinguishable in my memory from Gertrude Stein, that I was just waiting on an overdue payment from a well-known, highly respectable newspaper, and that I'd have the full amount for her the following week. While I lived there, I don't think I once paid rent on time. Eventually she kicked us out so her daughter could move in.

I spent much of that summer in music venues, in nightclubs, or at music festivals. I was typically there to work – reviewing, playing, organising – but the lines were blurred. I learned quickly that even a tenuous veneer of professionalism can open a lot of doors, so I never had to pay for anything. For the first time in my life, I had access. I had no money, so I didn't feel too bad about taking what I could get for free. I was thrilled by it too; the freedom to move around, to keep my own hours, to be present in places where I could never afford a ticket. The entire setup was liable to collapse at any minute, but its precarious nature made it exciting – surviving the uncertainty still brought an intoxicating sense of achievement then, like I had won through to another round in some addictive but unfathomable game. That feeling is well gone now.

What I remember most is the amount of talking I did that summer – I talked all day and all night; more than I ever had before, or have ever done since. I had a lot of freshly formed opinions and more than enough opportunity to convey them. I had an infinite appetite for connection at that time, and a taste for argument. I had the energy to care about the daily social grind of the circles I was running in, and a willingness to go against the grain in what I said. I criticised openly and without restraint. The music I was listening to, the events I was excited about, the institutions and people I derided – it was all fodder for my performative self-narration. I was talking myself up, talking myself into the role I imagined for myself. Like every other young idiot, I didn't realise yet how empty talk can be, and how little the noise of the night before really means by the morning after. Believing myself free of everything that had ever held me back, I was finally getting something I'd been craving for years – attention, excitement, involvement – and, for a few months at least, I couldn't get enough.

—

Coming home late most nights, I would walk back through the rows of neat, small houses between Camden Street and Clanbrassil Street, listening to Brian Eno's *Discreet Music* on my headphones. *Discreet Music* consists of two simple, three-note melodies played over and over again by a pre-programmed synthesiser. There is a lot of space between the repetitions, a space filled by the blurred and gradually decaying echoes of those same melodies. The echoes feed back into each other very slowly and very softly, a systemic recurrence and recombination which is well-defined from the outset, though its outline remains imperceptible while you're listening to it. It is constantly surprising.

Discreet Music persists for just under half an hour without any real development. It is a quiet, mellifluous piece that forgoes any progressive structure. It has no narrative, no dramatic punctuation. Its elements are immediately recognisable and they do not change until they have faded out once again at the end. It is more a state than a journey, purely atmospheric. Listening to it is like slipping into a crevice in time, finding yourself suspended.

I had never heard anything quite like *Discreet Music* before then, and it really took a hold of me during those summer months. It felt very much like a night-time record, a private world, somehow both mechanic and organic, systematic and deeply humane. Even though it was nothing more than a process in motion, it felt more alive, more spontaneous, more exciting than any other music I was hearing at the time. Its restrictions were self-imposed and somehow comforting. It didn't feel like a spectacle; like something to be consumed, or shared, or even talked about. When listening to it, my mind would wander without ever really escaping the music's particular muted shade; it coloured every thought. I internalised its atmosphere, that feeling of being inside of the music without ever feeling like you could understand it, or reach its bottom. Eno himself said it was more like a painting than music – it was just there, and you spent time with it. You came and you went; the music didn't change. Its reduction – almost absolute – spoke to a near-infinite set of possibilities; it felt like a boundlessly generous piece of music, open on every side. Walking home through the empty amber streets, quiet and alone after another night of endless talk, endless noise, it felt as if time had been dissolved, and I was caught in whatever nebulous cloud had settled in its place.

—

John Joe looked me in the eye when I arrived, and I don't know which of us was the more alarmed. He was shouting at his two nurses, and I was silent. I had no idea what to do. The desperation of the nurses, relying on me to improve the situation, was palpable. I felt an overwhelming desire to run away. John Joe had been, until this point, an authority figure in my life. In some ways, he was *the* authority figure: John Joe could tell even my father to do something and expect it to be done. Seeing him like this – confused, out of place, violent – I no longer had a clear idea where I stood with him. The positions we had always assumed were now reversed; I was being asked to take charge. Instead, I froze. For several minutes I stood there, completely lost, mumbling and looking for a way out. There was none.

—

I remember now: I fell in love that summer. I fell in love in that room, on the bed, by the blue of the window. Sometimes a love in its early days is indistinguishable from the quiet in which it takes root. That blue dark quiet.

—

I realised John Joe was trying to talk about the bog. June is the time of year when turf is brought home, and here he was, prone in his hospital bed, wondering how much of it had been done and how much more was left to do. I didn't know – I hadn't been home very much – but I made up whatever I could to keep him focused. Whatever would distract him from the presence of the nurses, whatever would take him away from this blanched, aseptic place. He seemed to think at times that he was actually on the bog, and not in a hospital at all. I tried to meet him wherever he was, tried to follow whatever winding paths he was travelling in his mind that afternoon. He would snap sometimes into a terrible awareness of his situation, and in each moment of clarity I could see the anger and fear swell inside of him. I held his arm if he tried to raise it when the nurses came near. He called them all sorts of names and I could do nothing about it. I thought of my parents on the motorway and counted each minute until their arrival.

—

At the tail end of that first free summer, I found myself in a cottage on the grounds of a large house in the countryside with some friends, who were all in a band together. The main house belonged to someone's aunt, and the cottage in the garden was empty; my friends planned to cloister themselves there for about six weeks with the intention of recording their first album. I went along with them to help out, as I had often done in the past. I can't recall what made this seem like a good idea. I'd gone to college to become a sound engineer, but that aspiration had faded by the time I'd finished. I didn't have much to offer my friends by way of expertise or advice, but I was envious of their proficiency, their ambition, and their gear, and I wanted to be a part of what they were making. This was the kind of thing I'd always wanted to do, and yet when the opportunity arose, I found I really had no good reason to be there.

I had begun to read the work of David Toop, an English musician and writer, and I carried his book *Haunted Weather* around with me while we stayed in that house. It's a book about music that pushes towards the edges of sense – quiet music, improvised music, music of long duration. Toop says that these kinds of musics, which force a heightened quality of attention on both the audience and the performer, are largely a response to the rhythms and structures of the natural world, an attempt to let that outside world permeate the music in some way. The composers and artists Toop discusses – Brian Eno among them – are trying to imagine different registers in which the music might more accurately or sympathetically reflect our experiences as people in the world, blurring the existing distinctions between the musical and the non-musical. Memory, reflection, vulnerability,

transparency – these are the touchstones of Toop's inves-
tigation. Long spaces between notes, such as you find in
Discreet Music, play on the fallibility of memory, asking
us to remember what has already happened while, at the
same time, straining our desire to find predetermined
patterns in everything. Music that resists familiar forms
asks its listeners to respond in an improvised, spur-of-
the-moment way. When we don't know where things are
headed, nothing can be decided in advance. We just have
to pay attention, stay with it, try to react in kind.

I was reading David Toop because, over the course
of that summer, I had felt something shift in my relationship to sound, to music, to the processes of memory
and invention involved in making and recording these
phenomena. I'm not sure it started with Richard Skelton,
whom I'd first heard that year, but *Landings* was certainly
a factor. Concepts and traditions I had previously taken
for granted no longer seemed to make much sense. I had
spent so many hours of my life up to that point trying, and
ceaselessly failing, to make music that explicitly detailed
my innermost emotions; my strongest, deepest passions.
This mostly meant writing songs about girls I thought I
loved, and how much I hated everything else. It worked
fine as therapy, but not so well as music.

Much of the music Toop talks about in *Haunted
Weather*, like *Discreet Music*, is generative: it comes out of
a process, grown from the bottom up rather than defined
from above. Eno describes making generative music as

being more like trying to create a seed than engineer a tree. I felt like I had been over-engineering trees my whole damn life, and I desperately needed to try something different.

Eno talks about how this kind of music opens outward from the composer's original idea, mutating and regenerating as it spreads. He discusses the theory of 'cellular automata', put forward by the physicist John von Neumann: the process by which even the smallest cell might evolve into something beautiful and unexpected. This opening out was so fascinating to me. It implied that the artist was just a starting point, and that the real magic would happen when the work came into contact with the world. It becomes the listener's duty not just to follow the composer's dream as a spectator, but to act as a conduit, to help bring it into being.

More than a little influenced by this idea – railing against the flaws I perceived in myself and my earlier methods – I began to resent the very idea of composed music, which I soon saw as arrogant and foolhardy. I took to wandering around the grounds of the country house with my portable recorder, popping balloons in the farmyard sheds, listening to the wind in the trees and the scratching of the dying plants against the windows of an abandoned greenhouse. I was trying to listen to the world as I found it, but really, I was seeking an escape from the grand construct of the record failing to be made around me.

The album we were trying to make was not unlike most others: a concrete list of songs, written over the course of

several years, to be preserved as a thematically and soni-
cally coherent whole. By unfortunate contrast, I had begun
to conceive of sound as something utterly contingent,
something unstoppable, illimitable. *Discreet Music* had
infected my thinking. The album my friends were making
demanded a type of perfection I had begun to distrust; I
had lost my faith in the idea of a perfect take, where the
recorded sound matches faultlessly with the sound we had
imagined in our heads. There seemed in this method very
little by way of discovery, or surprise. Recording instruments one by one, building up an album layer by layer,
you need to keep a clear picture of the whole in your mind,
to know where each piece of the puzzle is going to go and
how they will all fit together. I no longer believed such a
picture was really possible. Even if it was, I felt like that
picture would be no help to us.

I was thinking instead of sound as a function of the
atmosphere – emotional, social, climactic – in which it
is made and heard. I thought it was this totalised atmosphere we were responding to, whether we knew it or
not. I thought *this* is what we ought to be trying to record.
Everything else felt arbitrary. I thought that if we could
capture the atmosphere – the unrepeatable happenstance
of our being there, as a particular group in a particular
place and time – then the music would resonate with
everything which, to me at least, gave it meaning. All the
variables have to correspond for this to happen, this *rever-
beration*; from the placement of the microphones and the

choice of room to the emotional state of the musicians and the light coming through the windows.

This kind of coincidence is a by-product of patience and alertness. It's not even a question of waiting for the perfect atmosphere to come along; rather of recognising the characteristics of the one in which we find ourselves, and responding as suitably as we can to its affordances. I was beginning to develop something like an ethics of sound: could I be worthy of what was happening, what I was hearing?

This line of thinking did not make me a useful presence in that remote country house. I watched my friends work and felt a growing frustration at their approach. It felt like they were looking for something without opening their eyes: they had a fixed idea of what they wanted, and they set out to make that regardless of where they found them-selves. The sounds they made then were rarely listened to, but rather compared – held up against some ideal version they had in their heads. I felt this was holding them back. With all the tools at their disposal, with all the freedom in the world, they had built a wall around themselves. As far as I could see, nothing good would come of it.

Burned out, confused, lonely – I caught a lift back to Dublin. I had lasted about three weeks. The following day, my father was in Tallaght hospital for a check-up on a serious injury he'd sustained at work earlier in the year, and I was to meet him there for a lift back home. I knew my way around the hospital this time. I was sitting on a bench in reception when I got a text from one of my friends in the band, politely suggesting that maybe it would be best for everyone if I didn't come back.

—

Perhaps it is easy to see both the beginnings and the ends of things, but harder to know which is which at the time. John Joe's memory was already slipping when he entered the operating theatre that morning, but the occasion marks for me the real beginning of his troubles with dementia. The most simple and most selfish reason for seeing that day as a starting point is that it was also the beginning of my personal involvement with those troubles. Never before had I been asked to step so fully into his world.

It was my job that afternoon to be familiar, to help him find his bearings in an acutely unfamiliar situation. I was asked to be an anchor. It was my job to recognise him for who he was, and to give him the tools with which to recognise himself in that alien environment. The nurses, for all their strength and kindness, could not make him feel at home. They couldn't talk with him as if they were sitting by the range in his kitchen, or make him feel as if this was a day no different to any other. This was what he needed, and what I was unexpectedly tasked with providing. Trying to piece himself back together as the anaesthetic drained from his body, he reached for the building blocks of his identity and found them missing, or broken. He desperately needed someone to help him recover them. I was the only one around. He needed a mirror, someone to say: here you are, I see you. Only then could he reassemble himself.

It is easy, from here, to see that day as the beginning. Without realising it, I began a project – a shaky, unpredictable, overwhelming project – of trying to record John Joe in whatever ways I could. To track the situation in which he found himself, to follow it in a way that was not rigid, not predefined, but entirely sympathetic, alert to the contours and pressures of his particular atmosphere. It was some time, years really, before I realised that the pretentious theory of sound that I'd cooked up in that country house could have had quite practical applications in listening to, and caring for, someone who was losing their memory. These questions of recognition, of an adequate response to the demands a situation makes – if I'd had all that clear in my mind when I visited John Joe in hospital, maybe I wouldn't have been so childish and quiet. Maybe I wouldn't have been so scared. But I didn't have it then, and nothing at all felt clear. Even now it is easier to talk about the repercussions of these thoughts in terms of one's love of music, rather than one's love of people.

That summer, when I was young and free of every restraint, liberated for the first time from every tie and bond, I somehow became caught up in my grandfather the way one gets caught in rain. The rural, family life which had seemed before to be a restriction and a limitation became, to my surprise, an opportunity, and then an obsession. John Joe was like a gale force wind I was unable, or unwilling, to resist. I just went along with him, back the direction I'd come. I realised in those days that I wanted to record him as I would a most precious and enthralling sound, like a passing vibration in the air. If that day was the beginning of this project, it was in some sense the beginning of the end also. I could sense, even then, that what followed that trip to the hospital would not be good for John Joe, and would not be reversed. I wanted to listen hard to his final emergence; to capture his life in the last stage of its becoming – to record that person still forming even as he began, contrapuntally, to unravel.

a kind of
closing cadence

The older you get, in a sense, the more you forget. Vast tracts of your life sort of vanish in oblivion. But that which survives in your mind acquires a very considerable degree of density, a very high degree of specific weight. And of course once you are weighed down with these kinds of weight, it's not unlikely that they will sink you.

—W.G. Sebald

I went to Seamus Heaney's funeral. His work had meant a lot to me, so I wanted to mark his passing. I also wanted to see what the funeral of a national figure was like – I'd never been to something like that before. Anyway, the church was just a short walk from my flat. I was twenty-two and unemployed. I had the time to spare.

I got up after Niamh went to work. I showered, shaved, and deliberated too long over what jacket to wear. I had nothing in black, only a ratty brown thing that was worn thin at the elbows and coming apart at the shoulders. I took a photo of myself in the mirror and sent it to Niamh to get her advice. Walking around nervously that morning, I felt as I always do before formal occasions – inadequate and under-dressed, an imposter.

It was a warm and blustery day in September. Some lines had appeared in my head that morning, and I repeated them to myself as I made my way through the quiet suburbs of south Dublin:

> *I'm going to a funeral,*
> *And you are going to Bellaghy.*

Even though I had never written poetry, I felt inspired by the occasion and thought that I might work the lines into a poem when the whole thing was over. I made sure to take special notice of the unusual; the grown man pushing himself uphill on a child's scooter, the window-washers hanging off the roof at the Herbert Park Hotel, dark little figures half a mile up. This is what a poet does, I thought.

I crossed the roundabout outside the church and entered the queue to get through the side door. There were cameras everywhere. A book of condolences at the entrance seemed to exert its own kind of gravitational pull. I scribbled my name for posterity and added *Codladh Sámh*, which I saw someone else had already written but, feeling no need to be original, considered ideal for the job at hand. I had nothing of my own to contribute, in any case.

When I finally got inside the church there was standing-room only and not much of that. I leaned awkwardly against a wall next the entrance to the parish shop. I turned my head to see postcards and religious trinkets on little stands, holy water stacked on shelves like air freshener or shoe-spray. Aware that I was probably blocking the view of someone much more deserving, I slouched down as far as I could. I was able make out thin tufts of white hair peeking from the tops of cotton white robes on the altar, and an indistinct congregation down the main aisle. The place was lit up like a film set, the solemnity of the event somewhat infiltrated by its spectacle.

—

Heaney always reminded me of John Joe, in a way. They were of similar age, and they looked alike. Their lives turned out very differently but they came from the same world of small farmers in out-of-the-way places. Mossbawn felt like home to me, and these parallels helped make the poetry vivid and recognisable. I think sometimes that the only real difference between the two men was education. I see Heaney as someone who learned to question his inheritance, who went away on his scholarship and was never quite able to come back. Though half his siblings emigrated, John Joe lived his whole life in his father's house and never even left the country. But of course it's never so black and white.

For me, Heaney's success was evidence that the kind of inconsequential rural place I knew best could still be worth writing about, and that the touchstones of my parochial upbringing could be made relevant, even telling. It also showed me that my relationship to that place need not be straightforward. Heaney wasn't quite like the family and community he depicted in poems about his early life. He came from them, but he wasn't one of them, not exactly. He was a farmer's first son, but he was a Harvard lecturer too. It was only when he'd moved on that he found his imagination was still rooted in the place where he was born and raised. When writing about that home, he displayed a conflicted self-awareness I immediately understood. In his poems, memories of that place, and those people, are played back like records. Heaney drops the needle on a thin wedge of frozen experience and suddenly it erupts into life on the page.

I thought once that Heaney had negotiated some union in his life, some synthesis of the erudite poet and the hard-working man of the land. It looked as if he'd found a way to balance these different sides of himself, and to live in peace with both. I believe now that I was wrong, and he never did manage this. But I think it was that failure that produced his best work – the most complex, the most ambivalent, the sharpest. What he left as a child he left forever, and it lived only in memory and verse for the rest of his life, a tug on the string of the mind.

It seems to me that Heaney spent his career responding to that tug on the string. When I'm feeling optimistic, I think it was a way of being thankful for what he'd been given; a way of honouring it, and of keeping it with him. But I think there is guilt there too, and later a wishful escapism. Whatever its motivation, Heaney's writing forms a record of his relationship with home as it changed over the course of his life, an accretion of knowledge, significance and effort – solid and evidential. I can imagine the weight of it, of what one has said and believed to be true. In writing it all down, we give it shape outside of ourselves, and are charged then with carrying it with us always – this separate, uncanny thing that one no longer has the freedom to forget.

—

When I was still in college, Heaney published his final collection, *Human Chain*. My mother bought a copy, which I quickly stole for myself. The poems are quietly concerned with death, and with what it is like to live, for another short while at least, through the passing of one's friends and peers. It was a subject I could sympathise with, having seen Nana and John Joe suffer so many similar losses. My grandparents bore that pain with dark humour, lump-in-throat reminiscence, and the occasional moment of depression. *Human Chain* is woven from the same material – a collection that looks backward, finding what consolation it can in the images and sounds that swim up from the past.

By this time in his life, having survived a stroke and been fitted with a heart monitor, Heaney's memories of childhood were at their most distant and most precious. In 2009, shortly before *Human Chain* was published, Marie Heaney told the writer Robert McCrum that Mossbawn was her husband's paradise. 'His Eden,' she said. 'All he's ever wanted to do is go back.' I think those memories of Mossbawn – full of fresh-cut grass and benevolent skies; the taste of picked berries and the touch of insects – are for him an escape both from death's shadow, and from the labour of the writer. They push back against the inevitability of what Heaney called 'a kind of closing cadence' in his life, and they offer an alternative to the writer's duty of bearing witness; of noting down, connecting, drawing out – the responsibility, in the end, of always finding the right words.

The longing to be free of this endless task – or, more depressingly, the eclipse of the task's significance by the prospect of death – gives rise to a pastoral fantasy where language and the natural world are more intimately and unquestioningly sewn together. Words spring, simultaneously and without affectation, from each impression of the world. In *Human Chain*, Heaney is remembering a time where memory itself was not important, where names were given and narrative not yet established. A time or place when all of us were not so busy telling ourselves the stories of our own lives. He's dreaming of an open field while walking in a graveyard.

In these final poems, I can feel Heaney yearning for a world where meaning is to be found in the vitality of the experience itself, not in any use that might be made of it. A world where intuition is the limit of understanding, where whatever came, came naturally, and where there is little use for poetry at all because poetry is in everything and not separate from it, like it is for most of us. Living out the end of a life, burdened like a cart-horse by the weight of knowledge and experience – compounded in turn by the suspicion of their futility – I can imagine how this dream of an existence without inheritance, without record, without consequence, might come to seem like paradise.

—

My great-aunt Chrissy left home at fourteen to go join a convent. That was in 1954. The following year she went with her fellow initiates to America. I'd always assumed that, being the youngest of eight children in a fairly poor family, she'd been forced to go. But when I asked her, she told me that she chose to leave, and that she found the idea of a nun's life 'adventuresome'.

Chrissy was an intelligent kid, and her mother – a forceful woman, with real ambitions for her children – had pushed her to skip some years in school. But she felt lost among older kids, studying things she was too young to fully understand. She said that she felt shame and guilt over her struggles in school, and she was looking for a way out. It was true, too, that there wasn't much room for her at home. 'I did not have a voice and learned early it was better to be seen than heard,' she said.

In the final years of his life, the memory of Chrissy's departure for America really tortured John Joe. He could not bear to be reminded of it, and would sometimes be moved to tears if it crossed his mind. Sixty years after the event, he could still clearly recall standing with Chrissy in the yard at the back of their house, holding her hands on the morning she was due to leave. He remembered that she was a little girl in a brown skirt. They stood at the back door. They embraced, she was driven away, and it was thirteen years before they saw each other again. 'A lot of life happened during those years that I wasn't privy to and was barely made aware of really,' Chrissy told me. 'Everyone was so busy in their lives, raising children and marrying and all of that.'

This memory stayed with John Joe long after most others had disappeared. He would tell the story in snatches, and I only caught its outline. He must have thought about that day a lot in the intervening decades, and now he was replaying the scene over and over in his rapidly emptying mind. As his brain calcified and his other memories vanished, this story expanded to fill the newfound space. Each detail became magnified in front of him – where they had been standing, what was said, what happened next. He hovered over each of these points, reiterating them, binding them tighter to himself. John Joe could recall so little of his early life by then that this memory was a precious weapon in his battle against the void.

Shortly before John Joe was forced to give up driving, Chrissy came home for a visit. He brought her around in his jeep – to the bog, to the houses of old, mostly departed friends, and to the graveyard, to see their parents' grave. Chrissie told me how proud John Joe was of the new gravestone he'd erected there, how important that marker was to him. There is a photo of them there, standing by the grave with their sister, Josie. When they got home, John Joe took Chrissy outside to the yard and, standing where they'd stood over half a century earlier, told her about the tender memory he'd been harbouring all that time, welling up at the effort of recounting it for her. Chrissy listened and did her best to lighten this burden he'd assumed: really it wasn't such a big deal, it wasn't his fault, and anyway it was all so far in the past, almost a whole lifetime ago.

Chrissy had stayed with the convent for twenty-one years, getting a college degree and teaching children. During that time, her life was practically pre-arranged. 'You just went with the flow of things and the flow of life and rules and regulations and work and all of that – you just went with life as it was laid out,' she said. Eventually, in her mid-thirties, she tired of the routine and left that world behind. She found new friends, and partners. It wasn't easy to readjust to civilian life – she said that she was fifty before she felt like she'd grown up. 'I felt like I fitted in my skin and felt like I was my own person.' Work, she said, was very important to her. She earned herself a master's degree in psychology, and spent forty years working as a mental health professional with deprived communities, prisoners, and war veterans.

Chrissy never told John Joe that his memory was wrong. She didn't tell him what she later told us: that all those precious details did not tally with how she remembered things; it couldn't have happened that way. She couldn't have been wearing a brown skirt. She wasn't a little girl. In truth she had no memory of saying goodbye to him at all. 'It didn't make any sense to me in some ways because if he was saying I was a little girl in a brown skirt and came out to say goodbye to him, or to tell him that I was going to America, then why would you have let me go?' she said. 'But it was in his memory, for whatever reason. If there was a delusional quality to it, so it was. He may have been grieving a little bit about me going away so young, and maybe there should have been some intervention in the family. But I don't know. We didn't talk about deep things.'

There were surely differences in detail between John Joe's memory of that day and what actually happened, but the most important alteration was in its significance. For Chrissy, it was just a minor point in a narrative that began before that day and continued long after. For John Joe, it became a painful, unforgettable division in his life. Every time he drew the memory out, he had to reconstruct it, to tell the story to himself again, re-inscribing it as something he could remember, something he could rely on. But, like all memories, the details of this one shifted unnoticeably in the silence of its intervals, each recollection coming out altered in some small way until finally it was like a different memory altogether. John Joe had recalled his sister's leaving so many times, and over such a long period, that it became mostly fiction. Chrissy no longer recognised that story. 'We all see things not as they are, but as we are,' she told me. 'Sometimes it's more about us than it is about the other.' John Joe had never clocked that slow deviation, and so when most other memories had vacated his mind, a life's worth of regret, love, and shame rested uneasily upon the delicate frame of this departure.

—

I think the most important word in Heaney's poetry is 'between'. It's there all along, from the first poem to the last collection. Between the moment and the recollection of it, between the experience and the record of it – I think that's where Heaney lived. Neither fully in the present nor wholly in the past, ferried between the shores of each by the leaky craft of memory. The idea implies movement, traversal, and attrition. I think Heaney understood. There is no perfect recollection; you must leave something behind.

To be in-between is to be open to possibility and to change. But it is also to be doubtful, to suspect, to question. *How should a poet properly live and write?* That was Heaney's question. I ask it with a different inflection: how can I properly live *and* write? Writing divides us from life, in a small but permanent way. We can come close to it again, very close sometimes, but we must always return to whatever shadow of life this is; our life reconstructed from memory, where we carry our truth around with us and display it for others. Writing, for me, means that I cannot live in my father's house. And I cannot leave it either. I must be in-between, ready to preserve what I can, to make use of what I find. When the time comes, will I also long for the escape of imagined childhood, or some other warm oblivion? Heaney on one side, my grandfather on the other. Two paths. I ask as if it were a choice.

I went to Heaney's funeral as a writer, not as a mourner. I wasn't moved by a sense of loss or duty, or any great feeling at all; I just thought it would be something I could work with later on. I went to observe and to take notes. I knew this bit of life would make for good material.

—

The event of Chrissy's leaving is lost. John Joe's memory of what happened was different to the little Chrissy herself could recall. My memory of John Joe's version was thoroughly inaccurate – I needed Chrissy to clear it up for me. My recollection of Chrissie's version is partial at best. My attempt to record each variation, to piece together an accurate account, was flawed from the very beginning. There are as many versions of the story as there are tellings, and what I've written here is no more true or honest than any other. The difference of course is that this one will last; it will not be so easily forgotten. In some distant future, when I have cause to think of it again, I will look to this record for confirmation. It is written and, unlike memory, it will not fade. For better or worse it will become my truth. I will have to live with that.

There is some consolation in knowing that the effect of forgetting is not freedom or lightness. Or if it is lightness, then it is the lightness of a boat in a storm. John Joe spent years being blown between the familiar and the unfamiliar, tilting inexorably towards the latter. This buffeting was disorientating and frightening. In that kind of environment, it is natural to seek out anchors to steady us, life jackets that will keep a head above water.

The memories that John Joe retained, like Chrissie's departure, grew ever more important in this way. A few lucid scraps developed an intolerable density, just as words might in the lines of a poem. More and more meaning accrued around them because there was nothing else there. This density lead to a great degree of pain, particularly for my grandmother. John Joe's reliance on Nana was absolute; she was the most important anchor, so she bore the majority of the strain. The physical and emotional labour involved in being that anchor was considerable. He needed her to be there, and without her he was lost. As his life faded away, he belonged only to the house and to her. Only dying could return him to the world.

shelter

I

I was standing on Hiney's Corner and it was raining black and loud. Trying to keep one eye on the street, I sheltered in the window set into the front of Hiney's pub. The recess was about eighteen inches deep, usually enough to keep you dry, but the rain was coming down sideways and I was getting drenched.

It was a familiar spot – I'd worked behind the bar here for a couple of years during secondary school, and used to spend my breaks standing in that recess with friends or customers, watching the street and breathing in other people's cigarette smoke. The pub had changed hands a few times in the seven or eight years since I'd finished school and left for university. There is an awkwardness to knowing a place better than anyone there knows you.

On the rare occasions when I found myself back in town, I would sometimes get an embarrassed thrill from being served without recognition in the local Centra by someone I'd spent years sitting beside in class.

As I stood soaking on the corner, I had occasion – not for the first time while on assignment down the country – to reflect on the ignominy of being a journalist who doesn't drive. My mother had dropped me off on the way to the hospital with my grandmother – Nana was getting her bloods done – and I was waiting for Tom to come pick me up. Tom was the father of a guy I went to school with; he was also one of the people behind a local amenity known as the Lough Boora Parklands. I was writing about the Parklands for a glossy rural-affairs magazine, and I'd arranged to interview Tom at the site. Of course, I'd had to ask him for a lift too.

By the time I got into his car, wet all the way through, I was sure there was no way this man was going to take me seriously. Tom was about sixty and he spoke in a calm nasal drawl. I explained the work I was doing, and why I was interested in writing about the Parklands. I knew that the whole area had once been under water: the bed of a lake that covered much of Ireland's central plain. Then, in the aftermath of the last Ice Age, lake mostly gave way to bog. Much later, from the beginning of the twentieth century, most of the water that remained in the bog was drained away by the machine labour of industrialised peat manufacture. The sodden earth of the bog became dry, milled peat, which was drawn across the bed of the vanished lake in thin, beaten-up trains and used as fuel in the adjacent Bord na Móna power station.

The bog's usefulness as an energy source has now been exhausted, at least in Boora. One of my earliest memories from growing up around there is of being with my father in his van and watching from some distance as one of the power station's two giant chimneys was demolished by controlled explosion on a December morning in 1999. The chimneys were broad and round at the bottom, and curved gracefully upward to a height of eighty metres. In such a flat landscape, they had dominated the horizon for miles in every direction. If we happened to drive past them, I would crane my head out the rear window of the car, struggling to take in their immensity. For a long time, probably until they disappeared, they were the biggest structures I'd ever seen. When I began to work in Hiney's some years later, I discovered a series of three large photographs hung along one of the walls: the first depicted the chimneys in the moments before the explosion, the second captured the collapse, and the third showed just one chimney next to a void of smoke and rubble. The second would fall, in a similar way, a few months later.

In the late 1990s, Bord na Móna was selling off land reclaimed from the spent bog, and actively looking for new uses for that land. They secured government funding to create a number of artificial lakes for anglers. Encouraged by this support, Tom and his team put together an 'integrated land-use plan' that would include 'farming, forestry, amenity, and recreation'. In the years that followed, they gradually developed the park to meet their vision.

I first visited the Parklands as a teenager on a school trip, three or four years after the power station had been torn down. Tom had been our guide that day too. Back then, the park still felt like an industrial bog: Bord Na Móna was still in the early stages of figuring out how to manage Boora's transition to post-industrial life. Tom led the effort to plant forests, install cycle paths, and foster biodiversity. In time, the area became a haven for rare birds and insects, and packs of joggers swarmed through it on weekend mornings. What had been, for the guts of a century, an open-air industrial site for the production of milled peat was now a place for art, exercise, and wildlife. It was one example of what a post-industrial Irish landscape might look like, hinting at how the twentieth century's strategies for economic expansion might be picked apart safely in the twenty-first. Or at least that was the pitch I'd made to the glossy rural-affairs magazine.

—

Tom and I had our chat in the visitors' centre, which had just opened. It was a small, clean building with white walls, plate-glass windows and well-marked exits. We each had a cup of tea in the café staffed by two teenage girls, and looked out across a small lake known as Loch an Dochais, or 'Lake of Hope'. It was too wet to see much, but in the middle of the lake I could make out a sculpture of tangled metal rising out of a clump of reeds.

When I'm speaking with someone like Tom, someone with a wealth of practical experience in a field I know next to nothing about, I'm worried that I will sound ignorant, arrogant, or childish. To counteract this, I tend to over-prepare. I do extensive research, and make long lists of possible questions. The more nervous I am, the more work I make for myself.

With Tom, I tried to get into every aspect of the Boora project. I wanted to know the full history of the place. I asked him about every group or organisation that used the Parklands for their activities: astronomers, entomologists, boy scouts. I wanted to hear about the funding strategies, the environmental issues, the commercial relationships, everything. I could tell that Tom wasn't really used to being asked the kinds of questions I was asking him – he confirmed my suspicion a few weeks later, when he and his wife bumped into my parents in Hiney's – but his enthusiasm for the whole project was obvious. He'd been working on it for almost twenty years.

The interview soon wrapped up and I had a bit of time to kill. The rain had eased to a drizzle and I decided to wander around a bit while I waited for my lift home. I walked down past the birdwatchers' hut, and around the far side of the smaller lake. The only people about were a handful of fishermen, clad head-to-toe in waterproofs. Beyond the lake there was a clearing, with picnic tables, portaloos, and a strangely shaped pavilion made from repurposed materials – mostly long ESB poles of pitch pine and bolts of scrap metal from the Bord na Móna workshops.

Some of the works in the sculpture park were designed to be permanent, weathered landmarks. Others were conceived as temporary, and many of these more perishable pieces were just left to disintegrate naturally under the assault of wind, rain and plant growth. The last time I'd been to the park, there had been a great round tangle of willow branches arranged by an American sculptor, Patrick Dougherty. The light would come through the branches in soft bursts and the smell of the woven bark, ten tonnes of it rotting imperceptibly, hung in the air. I wanted to walk through it now in the gentle rain, circle around within it, the wattled walls bending always inward, tricking the eye and closing in gently on my body. But the piece was gone – Dougherty's creations typically have a built-in time-limit, and this one had been taken down some weeks before I arrived.

Walking around in the drizzle, it seemed to me the remaining sculptures had grown roots: compared to the first time I had seen them, ten years before, they were now more like outgrowths than implants. As time had passed, it had come to feel like they belonged. Surrounded by trees and watched over by stone-grey clouds, Eileen

McDonagh's 'Boora Pyramid' – an accumulation of large
granite slabs, stacked in a pyramidal structure about twenty
feet tall – felt like a monument raised by some extinct race
to long-forgotten gods. Like so many monuments of stone,
it felt anonymous and implacable and timeless.

—

My mother collected me from the visitors' centre and
Nana was in the car. All had gone well at the hospital,
and Nana was in a good mood, chatty and inquisitive.
As a young girl, she had often passed by Boora as she
cycled through the countryside around Rahan, the village
where she grew up, but she hadn't seen the place in many
years – not since before it was turned into a park. She
couldn't believe how much it had changed. Boora immediately became something beautiful in her mind, despite
the greyness of the afternoon.

I had spent most of my time since college living in
Dublin and writing about music for various magazines
and newspapers. I talked to second-rate indie bands who
were passing through Dublin on tour, and dissected
the minute differences between German techno records
which, to the less discerning ear, would no doubt appear
identical. I would occasionally meet people whose work
I really respected, and these connections, along with the
need to pay my rent, were enough to sustain my interest
in a job which, though sometimes boring and often

frustrating, nonetheless gave me an identity and a voice in my adopted city.

When I did come home, I had to answer the inevitable question about what I did for a living. I developed a straightforward reply: I write for a newspaper. This wasn't strictly true, but it suited everyone to keep things simple. My grandfather's Alzheimer's had been getting worse – John Joe could rarely remember who I was, never mind what I did for a living – and I think even Nana found it difficult to grasp the shape of my days. Lacking as I did any kind of position or routine, it was understandably hard for them visualise my life. To settle any concerns they had, I would seize upon events or details from my work that I felt could bridge that divide: a location I'd visited, a historical fact I'd come across, or even just meeting someone they might have known from television or radio.

When I got this gig with the rural-affairs magazine, the work became so much easier to explain. I came down from Dublin to profile a fiddle-maker who lived in the mill up the road from our house and I could tell them about it immediately, knowing they would understand. I talked to farmers with flooded farmyards; I assessed the state-of-play at Irish dairy co-operatives; I even wrote about cattle marts. Nana found the latter particularly amusing because she knew exactly how little I knew, or cared, about cattle marts. She thought it strange and fascinating, too, that someone like me, someone who had been to college and lived in a big city, would be writing about these kinds of things, the kinds of things she knew and cared about – they were too ordinary, too boring, or just not very smart.

As we drove the few miles home from Boora that October evening, I sat in the back and listened quietly to my mother and grandmother as they talked about the Parklands and the surrounding area, about the hospital they'd come from, and about the rivalry between our town's two undertakers – it looked like Nana's man was winning out. The sky cleared a little and turned an ardent red, softened by the fogged-up rear windows. Then it deepened into an inky blue, and night fell. It took no more than half an hour.

II

It was only when I stood up that I realised my foot had gone to sleep. I took a step forward, stumbled, and collapsed. While falling, I was more concerned for the safety of my laptop, which I was holding, than I was for myself. I hit the ground shoulder-first, laptop successfully protected, and moaned in pain. I had done something to my foot; perhaps it was broken.

A few days later I found myself limping around Boora with my parents, my foot still horribly swollen. It was late afternoon, April, probably Sunday. I had arrived the previous evening, on the way back from a literary festival on the west coast, where I'd been repeatedly forced to explain the cause of my lopsided gait. It was my mother's birthday that weekend, and we'd all had a bit to drink the night before. My dad was breaking in a new pair of runners and they were cutting his ankles. My mother had no physical complaints and just wanted some fresh air. We passed through the clearing with the picnic tables, past the sculptures and down the newly paved paths that cut through the managed forest of birch and pine.

We followed the signs and trail-marks to a surprisingly desolate spot right at the heart of the park. I had wanted for some time to visit the Mesolithic site, where the remains of fourteen campfires were found buried in the silty clay of Boora's ancient lakeshore. The remains were between 8,400 and 9,000 years old. Fires burned in those hearths less than a thousand years after the end of the last Ice Age, when the bog we were walking through had yet to be formed. The people who lit those fires were hunters. Game of any size was scarce on the island then, and the larger birds that lived around the lake were a rare source of meat. The archaeological evidence suggests they spent the summer in Boora, and lingered briefly into autumn. When the birds began to fly south, the hunters returned to the woodlands near the coast and prepared for winter. The cold was less extreme nearer the sea, and in the forests they could stockpile the nuts, berries, and grasses on which they would survive through the harshest months of the year.

The wind blew hard around the barren site. My foot was throbbing inside my boot. There were some small, upright stones and an information board to show you that this was indeed the place you were seeking: the place where, with a single archaeological discovery, the accepted date of human habitation of the Irish Midlands was pushed back by over 3,000 years. I was standing where some of the earliest human inhabitants of this island had once kept themselves warm, on the shores of a vast and now-vanished lake, and my father was muttering to himself about runners he'd bought in Aldi. It had been a long walk.

Tall trees soaked up the noise of the road and blocked the sight of the wind turbines beyond. With my back to the information board, looking out over what was once the lake, it was almost possible to imagine that no one had set foot in this place since those ancient hunters had extinguished their fires and departed for the coast. Though the landscape was now so different from the one they'd left behind, it felt to me like the place was waiting for them to come back.

I have always liked to imagine those earliest times, when the island was dark and no more than a few thousand people walked its still-uncertain paths. I am drawn to the quietness of it, and to the idea of an unknown wilderness that is both extensive and bounded. How wide the lake must have seemed when they set out in their boats, how deep and mysterious the forests which then covered most of the island. I like to think of the ancient wild cat whose remains were discovered between the hearths. I long to hear the voices of those first hunters, and to imagine the conversation at the fireside. They were the first people to make lives for themselves in this part of this country, when everything was new. I wonder who was the first to be born here, the first to live their whole life and die here.

I've tried writing these early hunters into stories, but the stories don't come off because I cannot close the gap between those strangers and myself. I don't know, and can't really imagine, their dreams, their desires. I find myself hovering somewhere above them, observing them, without ever being able to get close. I ask only the big dumb questions with no answers: what did they feel when they landed on the shore of this unmapped island, previously only glimpsed from across a narrow sea? Did they make each other laugh? How did they communicate joy and fear and hope? Did they feel safe here? Would what I mean by the word 'home' make any sense to them at all? I can push the figures around the board, but I can't put words in their mouths. They never talk back.

—

When I get nervous, I overcompensate. I fill all the gaps I see with information. I use any facts I can find to close the distance between me and what scares me. Nothing scares me more now than the distances I sometimes feel between me and my family, or between myself and the place where I was born. The direction my life has taken so far – my work, my friendships, the education my parents gave me;

an education they never received – has led me away from the people who raised and formed me, the places I have known and loved the longest. I left home because I felt like I was missing out on something I could only find elsewhere; a more diverse and cultured world. It was a good reason to leave, and a true one. But I keep returning now because I've realised that what I have at home is something that cannot be found anywhere else. By watching my grandparents fade, by listening to their lives and the lives of those around them, by watching my brothers grow up and leave in turn, I have been drawn back to a place which I recognise now as being on the edge of disappearance. I have a grim sense that the family and the life I was once so eager to outgrow might someday soon be gone, and there will be no one around to tell people what it was like to be there. My fear is that, in time, even I won't remember; that I will let perish something that cannot be replaced.

Short of giving up my current life and moving home, my strategy for staving off that destiny has been one of research and writing. I have tried to pay closer attention to my family's lives than I did when I lived with them. There aren't any secrets I hope to uncover, or family history I want to drag out into the revealing light of day. But I imagine I might, by accumulation of stories and points of reference, stitch myself back into the fabric of the place that I'd so desired to escape. I find myself looking for a conception of the place I come from that dissolves the distinctions I feel within myself, a story I could tell in order to feel singular, native, whole. I'm looking for roots, origins. I want to be from that place, and only that place; to be of those people, and only those people. I want to speak and be understood; to think along their lines. When everything around me seems arbitrary and directionless, when I have no idea what I'm doing, I dream of a great chain with a solid iron weight at the end, descending into the black. In writing towards my parents and my grandparents, in writing about the place where they live, I attempt to take them inside myself again, as it was when I was a child, when I knew nothing else. But writing does not grant me that kind of intimacy; writing, in the end, keeps us apart.

When I find myself in Boora, looking out across the absent lake and thinking about the vanishing point of human habitation – campfires in the dark and the vast, unknowable silence – I know that I have gone too far in my search for reconnection, that I have become lost and must turn back.

III

On Saturday evenings, Nana would go to mass with a neighbour. While she was gone, someone would sit with John Joe in their kitchen. If I was at home I would usually volunteer.

Our houses are down a dead-end bog road barely wide enough for a single car, a few miles from the nearest town. The quietness and the darkness of a winter's night there – when the lonely iridescence of the Sacred Heart in my grandmother's kitchen is visible from 200 or 300 yards away – has to be felt to be believed. Sitting beside the black iron stove in that old but comfortable kitchen, there was only so much work I could make for myself. I could boil the kettle and put more turf in the fire. I could search in the biscuit tin or, with rare luck, wash a few dishes. John Joe, murky with Alzheimer's, wasn't overly fond of the radio or television at that point, and we were not intimate enough to simply be quiet together. At times like this, you become painfully aware of how important the art of meaningless conversation can be, how a simple story can make the minutes fly, but I was never much of a storyteller. John Joe and I would talk about how good the new stove was – the previous relic having recently been consumed in a chimney fire – or where I was living in Dublin. There was always the weather, but I could barely squeeze more than a sentence or two out of that. I developed the dreadful sense that nothing I might say would interest him in the least.

It was in this setting that Boora became something of a life-saver. When I told John Joe that I had been working there that day in October, he took it to mean that I was working for Bord Na Móna, as he once had. For a time, this misapprehended fact became the sum total of my identity in his eyes. One evening, he was sitting silently in his chair by the fire, observing from some distance a small family gathering. I was sitting at the table, the nearest to him. Someone – probably Nana, because she often did this kind of thing – asked him if he knew who I was. He looked up at me and said, simply, *Boora*. I was happy to be recognised at all.

On our Saturday evenings together, John Joe would happily talk about his memories of working, for almost two decades, with Bord na Móna in Boora. John Joe's work there was seasonal; every summer the teams of local men would be given a quota of peat to produce. If the team met the quota by the season's end, they would be rewarded with bonuses. John Joe told me that I would make good money if I kept my head down and worked hard. To keep the conversation going, I said I'd use the money to buy a car. He told me to get a big one, a Merc, and run all the other fuckers off the road.

The money John Joe had made each year at Bord na Móna had got his wife and six children through some tough times – then as now, our small farm was not enough to really live on. He'd even got a meagre pension out of it after he retired. He didn't mind the bosses, he said: they were good men and they wouldn't mess you around. If you did your work, you got paid. Simple as that. He wondered if Tom, who'd been my guide, was the same Tom who'd been there in his time. I told him I wasn't sure, but I didn't think so. He asked me about other people he had worked with, wanting to know if they were still around. Even though I didn't know who he was talking about, I knew they weren't there any more. They were as old as him or older, all his old and vanished friends, and long finished with their working lives. Many were dead. I just told him I didn't know.

He spoke with particular vigour about his colleagues who weren't interested in work at all. These men – I can picture them so clearly – were always messing and breaking things, throwing things at each other in the workshops or playing practical jokes out on the cutaway. They were like class clowns; the boys who never grew up, never took anything seriously. These *blackguards* and *friggers* would resurface in his chat every few minutes. He liked a joke as much as any man, and possessed a beautiful, musical laugh, but he had no time for that nonsense. I don't think his anger towards them had anything to do with quotas or targets – it was just that he was there to work; he wanted to get the job done as well and as quickly as he could.

—

In truth, John Joe never worked in Boora. He worked in Blackwater, a bog near the banks of the Shannon, twelve or thirteen miles west of Boora. But at this remove, the distinction is of no consequence. The shapes those places took in our imaginations were momentarily aligned, and they opened up a tenuous connection. We could talk as adults about work, and this felt like a miracle.

I can't remember now how long it took for the association to fade. It wasn't long. I think I can remember one reference to Boora at Christmas that year, just two months later, but it was probably gone shortly after that. Nana contracted pneumonia the following February and spent a week in hospital. Though I passed many hours in the kitchen during that week, I don't recall it ever being mentioned.

fidelity

One can look at seeing; one can't hear hearing.
—Marcel Duchamp, *The 1914 Box*

May 23rd, 2016

Lying in bed on the top floor of an old apartment building, windows open to the morning, the sound of the street below is soothingly diffuse. Niamh is in the next room. We have been in Lisbon for three days. I take my phone from the bedside table and activate its voice recorder. I lie very still. The volume of the street seems to rise in a straight line until the sounds fill the air around me. I can hear the engines of the cars and buses outside. Students are coming and going from the medical college across the square; their graduation party took place the night we arrived. Beginning in the late afternoon, they gathered until the square was full of families and friends, food and drink; photographs, laughter. Each student climbed to the top of the steps at the entrance to the broad, stone building, where a man with a microphone waited for them. One by one, he placed an oversized hat on their heads, said a few words, and clapped them on the hat with a large staff. Everyone cheered. Niamh was asleep then, her head in my lap. We were in the living room, the television was on, muted. Our first night in the city – wine-drunk, exhausted. Outside, the cheering in the dark. It went on and on until, sometime around midnight, the crowd began to splinter off in smaller groups, disappearing down the narrow, cobbled roads.

Two days later, I can hear the crowing of the hens and ducks who have made the square their home. They wander about the grassy areas during the day, calling to each other and feeding from the scraps of passersby. At night they sleep in cages the city has built for them. I can hear the sounds of distant radios in cars, newsagents, and flats all around. It is quiet and continuous, the sound of the city, and I sink into it until it washes over me, as if every sound had its source right there in my room. The light linen curtains billow back and forth across the floor. Eventually the wave crests, and the sound fades away again. I reach for my phone. It has been just eight minutes, but it felt like an hour. When I listen to the recording – days later, back at home – I can hear nothing of what I experienced at the time. It sounds like any day in any city, heard from any room.

—

I began recording almost as soon as I began to write. I was maybe thirteen when I began to fill up copybooks with lyrics. I would practice the songs I'd written every evening after school, playing the guitar in my room and singing along in my head. I was embarrassed by my voice – I still can't hold a tune – and afraid that anyone would hear the words, which were pretentious and personal. My bedroom was plastered with posters of the usual rock canon, and I would sit there for hours alternating between my own songs and the songs of the bands I loved – those I could play along to at least.

Around this time, Nana brought home a book, a beginner's guide to recording music with a computer. It came bundled with a cheap black microphone. I don't know why Nana bought it – she had never used a computer – but my brother had bought his first drum kit by then, so maybe he'd asked her to get it. We had a family computer, installed in the corner of the kitchen, and a priceless dial-up internet connection. I spent hours downloading the free recording software the book recommended. We plugged the microphone into the back of the computer, and we were good to go.

The kitchen was neither the quietest nor the most private space in the house, but nonetheless I sat there with my headphones on, pointing the microphone at different parts of my guitar, and generally learning the ropes of the software. Once the sound was inside the computer, you could pull it apart; you could duplicate it over and over again, you could add effects, you could slow it down, chop it up, or reverse it. I quickly realised that what went in had only a tangential relationship to what came out. I realised that to record something accurately – to make something sound like my favourite albums – would be an immensely difficult task. I also came to see that recording music could be as creative and expressive as writing it; there was no limit to what you could do. Within a year or two, I had decided I would train to be a sound engineer.

Sound engineering is a technical trade, but there is a mystery to it as well. It's like writing in that respect, though you can say the same of almost any activity if you think about it long enough; there is always a point where the apparently simple blurs into the unknowable, where craft gives way to magic. Still, it's that mix of the practical and the mercurial that has kept me interested in the field for the last fifteen years.

Because recording is a sequence of decisions, and each decision will enforce its own subsequent constraints on future decisions, it's no exaggeration to say that everything matters. There is basically endless scope for debate with regard to technique, equipment, and even philosophical approach. I have seen this conclusion taken to its logical extremes: I read once of a studio where every single cable was tested to discover the direction in which it sounded best. We're talking miles and miles of cables, running underneath floors and along walls, tested, pulled up, reversed, and tested again. The results were compared (I can't imagine how minute the differences must have been), and the cables re-laid based on the engineer's assessment. I admire that kind of crazed perfectionism. There is something pleasingly luxurious about the whole idea, not just because it's expensive and time-consuming, but in how it reflects a belief in an abstract, almost self-negating purity; as if, with enough consideration, the whole recording apparatus might become so clear, so transparent, that it would disappear entirely. The kinds of engineers who go in for this remind me of the engineers who manufacture the giant glass lenses for the world's best telescopes – perfection is the minimum expectation.

When I was a teenager, I wanted to record everything well. I wanted to master the techniques that other engineers had used, because what most people want from a recording is a sound that already exists – either the sound they hear in the room, or a sound they've heard on another recording. Because there is always friction in the recording process, and because no two situations are ever exactly the same, learning how to replicate those other sounds is a necessary part of the apprenticeship for any sound engineer. You pick things up in the stories that other engineers tell – how a certain band got that beautiful drum sound; how one engineer mic'd a particular singer to get that ghostly vocal. You invest time, and money, because someone else always has better gear, and you're trying to catch up. You research the pros and cons of different microphones, and you learn how to position them just right. There is a great need for precision – you move a microphone an inch or two and the sound changes dramatically. You recognise the benefits of certain materials, the deficiencies of certain rooms. Eventually you learn – and this is often the last thing you learn – to listen.

—

Once, when I was still recording in the corner of my parents' kitchen, I could hear a quiet, irregular crackle coming through my headphones. I checked all my cables, I checked the settings on the computer, I checked the headphones and the speakers – I couldn't figure out where this sound was coming from. After ten or fifteen minutes of growing frustration, I realised I was picking up the sound of wood burning in the range at the other end of the room. This is the first instance I can remember of the world appearing unbidden in a recording of mine – a significant interruption.

—

Recording studios are, on the whole, extremely boring places. They are typically closed and carefully controlled environments. When I was in college, our studio was completely dead. There were two rooms: the control room, with the mixer, the speakers, and most of the other gear; and the oxymoronic 'live' room, which was a narrow, echoless box. You build rooms like these because you want to capture sounds with as little interference as possible. These rooms give you a lot of control over what you record, and they allow you to be sure of the consequences of your decision making – you can concentrate on the effects of your microphone choice and placement, and you can perceive the sound accurately as you tweak the frequencies. I understand why rooms like these exist, but I would never want to spend time in them.

I actively avoided the studio in college, preferring to do my recording projects at home. My brother and I had convinced my father to let us build a would-be studio in a corner of his shed, graduating from the cowshed at the back of my grandparents' house. The new studio soon expanded to fill most of the building. When we were finished, it had three rooms, including a nearly soundproof room for my brother's drums, and a control room for me and my gear. I had thrown myself into the planning of this studio, spending weeks reading books and researching on forums. I turned down a summer in London with my then-girlfriend in order to work on it. Instead, I followed the self-build studio projects of middle-aged guys from all across the world and tried to communicate what I was learning to my dad, who had signed up to actually construct the thing. I built acoustic panels that I could move around to control the sound in the rooms, without replicating the suffocating experience I'd had in college. I recorded my brother's bands, and my own. I advertised the studio on forums and social networks, and people actually paid me to record them. Some were teenagers, as I was, and others were twice my age. They drove to our house from all over. Sometimes, if they were nice, and if there weren't too many of them, my mother made them dinner.

For four or five years, I spent way too many hours in that shed. I'd come home for weekends and holidays and barely leave it. It was impossible to heat in winter. We bought space heaters, but they ran up my parents' electricity bills. I remember one night around Christmas when, unable to play guitar or even use my laptop, I ran back inside every half hour to warm my fingers by the fire. My brother would stay warm by playing the drums; I would sit in the other room, recording him, wearing three jumpers and two coats. It never bothered me. I'd stay out there half the night.

I enjoyed the feeling of control I had in the studio, and I got good enough at the job to capture what people would ask me to capture, but what I loved most was the freedom to experiment, and to lose control. There is something genuinely liberating about being in a space where no one can hear you. It was only in that room that I began to record my own voice, only there that I felt free enough to try things out. I sang, and sometimes I screamed – twice my father rushed in, expecting to find that I had electrocuted myself, or broken a bone. I told him I was just trying to record some vocals for a song. I was very into black metal at the time.

I liked putting microphones in unusual positions. I liked putting amplifiers and drums in unsuitable places. With my own studio, however basic, I had license to mess around, to see how something might sound if we didn't take the obvious route. Most of my favourite recordings mixed the two approaches: some elements would be immaculate, others would be strange and unexpected. Some natural and realistic; others distorted, synthesised, or out of whack in some way. I wanted some part of the result to be unintentional, or unimagined at the start. I wanted, more and more, for what I was making to be open to influences beyond me. I began to realise I didn't need a soundproof room any more. I loved my studio, but I could leave the doors open. I began to take my microphones outside.

—

December 29th, 2015

In the dead week between Christmas and New Year's, I give myself too much to do. I have packed my camera and my recorder, and I have decided I will make a film. Just a short film, very abstract, which will capture the landscape around our farm. It's the latest manifestation of an old idea, a project which I need, every few years, to recast in a different form.

I have been wandering around for hours each day, whenever the weather permits, collecting images and sounds. Today I am in the bog again, and the wind is blowing hard. I have brought two microphones and my recorder, but left my camera at home. I want to capture the sound of the wind as it blows across the high bank. I place my microphones about eight feet apart at the bottom of the round, red bush that stands alone on the higher ground. The sky is huge and grey and the colour has been drained from everything. I connect the microphones to the recorder, and activate its internal microphone as well. I hold the recorder in my hand, and stand between the mics on the ground, a few feet back, facing in the same direction.

Standing stock still on the high bank – headphones on – my mind begins, very slowly (so slowly that I do not notice it), to empty, to become quiet. For just a few, uncountable minutes, I stop telling myself anything. Thinking becomes a distraction. At the same time, I am not focused on anything specific. The sound in my ears is no different to what I would hear without headphones – just the bluster of the wind as it whips through the heather and, more distant, blurred, the branches of the trees at the bog's edge. I am alone in the centre of a faded brown island, raised above a surrounding sea of palest green. I have nothing to say here, not even to myself. I let the wind blow over me.

In a short time – I could not say how long – my eyes will begin to see again. My legs, without haste or aim, will move. I will be like a character in a film, when the colour emerges from monochrome and a still image suddenly ratchets into motion. I will begin to pack up. I will think: *I would like my ashes spread right here.* I will catch that thought and dissolve it. Move on. Why am I so morbid in this place? I can't help it. One's sense of time is so different here. Listening to almost nothing, I enter a world where it appears logical, for a brief moment, to think that I do not exist. When I wake, I think of dying.

—

When you record music on a computer, you are constantly aware of time. Whatever software you use, it will tell you how long you have been recording for. It will break the time up into whatever measures you choose – musical time: beats and bars; clock time: minutes and seconds; computer time: nanoseconds and samples; a minimum of 44,100 samples for every second of clock time. Smaller and smaller blocks allowing you to perfectly align, cut, and sequence your recordings. When a band records all their instruments separately, they play to a metronome so that everyone is in time with each other. If the drummer is bad, you edit the files and fix his timing. Everything is defined by its relationship to the grid, a flexible but ever-present frame of reference for the entire project.

The biggest difference I have found in recording outside the studio is the disappearance of this grid. When I'm walking around with my portable recorder, I'm not thinking about how the recording I'm making is going to line up with something I've already recorded, or will record in the future. Time is passing but it is, for the most part, irrelevant. I'm not paying any attention to it. This means there is much less pressure on whatever it is I'm recording. I'm content to wait, to see what will or won't happen. I know the events of the world will take as long as they take and there is nothing I can do to speed things up. Or to slow them down – I need to be ready for what happens, when it happens. The feeling is unlike any other: a heightened awareness of everything except time in the usual sense. You begin to understand events and sounds in relationship to each other, rather than by their adherence to an unflinching external clock. Minutes elongate, or disappear entirely.

The purpose of the grid, in studio recording, is to make things reproducible. You use the metronome so that performances will synchronise. You want to be able to play a recording over and over again until you build up everything you need around it. You want each recording to be accurate because every other recording will interact with it, and in some way depend on it. You want to be able to repeat, as closely as possible, the experience of hearing it for the first time, all at once. Without the grid, I find this is basically unachievable. Often the recordings I have made around home appear, on listening back, to be lifeless, or at least devoid of what drove me to make them in the first place. They go on for hours, and they contain so little – just the sound of the wind, some birds, maybe a river or the animals in the shed.

And yet, if I have tried to capture anything with my microphone and my recorder, it is that time when time itself is changed. I want to listen back and hear myself transported. I think that if I could get it just right – if I hold the microphone steady, if I barely breathe at all – one time would fold seamlessly into the other, and extinguish itself. I am thinking of Roland Barthes again, listening to a recording of himself playing the piano. 'The past of my playing would coincide with the present of my listening,' he wrote, 'and in this coincidence, commentary would be abolished.' There is just one difference: I am trying to listen to myself listening.

—

June 21st, 2016 (Midsummer's Day)
There is one house beyond my grandparents' place, beyond the turn for the bog, right at the end of our dead-end road. It belonged to John Joe's cousin, Kieran. He and his wife died some years ago, and the house has been empty since, the victim of a contested will. Sometimes when I'm home, I'll wander down there. I like it best at evening time because, from the field at the back of the house, you can see right down over the bog and the low light causes the land to glow. The house is falling apart. A sizeable block of stone has become dislodged from the roof at the gable end

and is caught up in a thick cable that runs along the wall. A television aerial sways precariously against the chimney. There is a car in the open shed, covered in leaves fallen from the trees around it. A window at the back of the house has been smashed and the glass lies shattered on the ground outside. Inside the empty frame is the kitchen sink, replete with rusted taps, mouldering tea bags, and a half-full bottle of washing-up liquid. On the windowsill, next to an unopened jar of honey, there is a porcelain statue, about four inches tall, of two hands clasped in prayer. The countertop is littered with cups and plates.

I don't touch anything. Though I was often inside the house as a child, I wouldn't open the door and walk around the rooms now. Time is too still here. I feel out of place. Life has stopped and there is no immediate sign of it stirring again. I don't want to interrupt that stillness, or intrude upon it. I stand back a little, take out my recorder. I close my eyes and press record.

The recording is weak. Sound alone cannot capture the entropy; it cannot show the crumbling walls and the swaying aerial, or the way the evening sun catches the blossom by the shed. If I were to describe it to you in words, this place, and play you the recordings I've made, you would not see it as it was. 'Sound may say – these are the invisible traces of memories that have collected over centuries; this is the unique atmosphere of this precise spot,' writes David Toop. I want that to be true of this place, not just of my listening here but my listening back too. I wonder what I would have to do to make this 'unique atmosphere' available to others. I resort to description, or to photographs – eye-witness accounts. But the sound of this derelict house, the pressure in the air here, evades capture or documentation. Listening in the back yard, I can feel a great and terrifying pause. Sound is a medium of time; it unfolds. When I'm standing there, it feels like time has stopped. How can I record that?

—

Years ago, I thought that what I'm writing here would be best done through sound. I wanted to record the landscape where I grew up, and where John Joe had lived his whole life. I thought that if I could record the fields and the bog, this specific and circumscribed location, then I would capture something of the people who live there. I hadn't yet thought to record them directly. I believed that the ambience would be enough to show someone my home. This, I suppose, is an ideal of field recording, a notion of atmosphere and transference.

I did eventually make a record, or rather a tape, with the recordings I'd made, but I smothered them in noises of my own – thick drones, buzzing distortion, feedback. Occasionally you could hear the birds, or a van pulling into the yard of our house, or some muffled conversation, but I knew that I hadn't got what I'd set out to capture in those recordings. I was still thinking – like I had as a teenager

– that I could record anything. I thought that I could describe a few square miles of land with nothing more than a cheap portable recorder. I was relying on a version of that old tangential process, hoping that what went in – quiet, empty hours – would reappear, on the computer, as a deep and meaningful story. Even though I recorded everything except what I thought was important, I nonetheless thought that what was important would be obvious, just because it was obvious to me. I thought everything would just be there, apparent to everyone. Needless to say, the effort was a failure. I can hardly listen to it anymore.

I am only now realising that I can't show people what it's like to hear something, least of all something as vague and disparate as a landscape. Listening is not something I can share with people in other times and places; not as I would with a camera, or with words. Hearing is so constant, it locates us in a world more extensive even than sight, and yet it operates on a secondary level most of the time – somewhere beneath thought, fleshing out but rarely supplanting the visible world. Even at its most direct, sound suggests, it doesn't show. The project of recording these last few years required something that sound alone could not provide. So much of what I wanted to tell you could not be caught on tape. The time of memory is altogether different to normal, everyday time, and it can't be shared in the same way. It doesn't inhabit the same kind of space or shape. Unlike the passing of time, which you hear whenever you listen to anything, memory is inaudible – it takes place along a hidden, interior wavelength. Belonging is not something that one hears on the air. I am talking, I suppose, of depth. Of all the times other than the time that I am recording now.

—

My favourite sound is of the horses in the field next my parents' house. Sometimes, in the very middle of the night, I can hear them running, two or three of them, down the hill in the centre of the field. I crack my window and listen. Unadjusted to the moonlight, my eyes cannot make them out. They sound like rain in the distance, low and intimate in the dark. Once or twice I've placed my recorder on the windowsill and tried to capture the sound, but it's impossible. My tools are rudimentary; the distance is too much. I think of what it would take to record it adequately – the nights spent waiting for the right conditions, the patience and the expense, and most of all the skill you'd need, when it does finally happen, to preserve that most vital frequency: the sudden, surprising blush of wonder.

—

August 8th, 2014

I get comfortable on the warm black wrapping that covers the round bales stacked at the back of the farmyard. I have placed my recorder on another bale, out of sight. I settle in to watch the sunset. We played on bales just like these as children; climbing up, jumping from one to the other, slipping our tiny bodies through the gaps between them. I can smell the plastic in the sun. I look out at the trees across the narrow road and listen to the activities of the birds who live there. I can hear the cattle lowing as they always do in the evening. I never noticed the sound when I was younger, not until a visiting friend pointed out how loud it was. I can hear the rapid pulse of the drain that runs underneath the farmyard and reappears at its rear gate, twenty yards from where I'm sitting. From here, the sun will fall behind the trees and disappear, later than you'd think, off behind the bog; closer to north than west. The sky glows orange and pink, then a bruised blue. When the sun is gone, it is completely dark, and silent. Only when the clouds are low can you detect the light of the nearest town reflected in the air above you.

I heard my mother coming before I saw her. I heard boots on the concrete, the opening and closing of gates. She climbed up and sat beside me on the bale, watching the sun while we talked. I can't remember much of what we talked about, only that she mentioned how peaceful this spot was, and I replied, *Yes, I know, that's why I came out here.*

When it came time to go back inside, when we'd finally had enough of the midges, I went to grab my recorder. *Were you recording this whole time?* she asked. I had been, for almost two hours. My mother was worried that the talking had ruined the recording. I told her it didn't matter because I'd probably never listen to it. The recording was just an excuse to sit quietly in one place, a way of doing nothing. A way of being alone with myself. I could continue listening to it now and tell you what we talked about then, my mother and I, but I'd rather not know. It was just chat, just passing time.

pneumonia

I caught the last train of the day to Tullamore, where my father and his sister met me at the station. It was a dark and cold evening in early March. As soon as I sat into the car, I could tell they were worried. They had just come from the hospital. My grandmother had been admitted that morning with a particularly harsh dose of the flu. She'd become increasingly worn out over the previous few days and her growing exhaustion prevented her from fighting off a common cold which, by the time the ambulance arrived to collect her, had escalated to the brink of pneumonia. In the car, my father was shook. He talked about the moment he entered the ward and saw her there, her tiny frame beneath the white bed sheets, tubes attached to her face and arms, her eyes closed. He said he thought for a second that she was gone, or soon would be.

We drove home in the dark. My aunt called her sister in Chicago and told her what was happening. That sister had spent most of the winter in Ireland and had just recently returned to her home and husband in America. She was debating now whether she ought to turn around and fly back here again. There was genuine concern that Nana might not make it, and that there would be no chance to see her again. Three of Nana's children live in America, and as we navigated the familiar roads, I could feel every inch of that distance. I was glad then to be just a short train journey away. The thought of having to weigh up a transatlantic flight – the time, the money, the energy – against the risk, however slight or uncertain, that you would never see your mother alive again – it was terrifying. Of course you would want to go, but I could easily imagine myself delaying the decision, prevaricating, waiting for some sign that it was indeed the right time, and that I simply had to go *now*. I felt certain that, if I found myself in that situation, I would be in the air when it happened, and I would arrive too late.

With Nana in hospital, John Joe was alone. This was the reason I'd come home. I was volunteering to take my share of shifts in the round-the-clock care he would need while Nana was away. My father decided that he would spend the nights there, sleeping in the spare bedroom. When he left for work in the morning, my mother would take over for an hour or two. My aunt came after her son had left for school, and my mother went to work herself. I was there to give my aunt a break during the day, to free up a couple of hours so that she could go home and clear her head. I think if she'd been forced to stay there all day, without interruption, she would have quickly gone mad. Anyone would. Those midday hours were hard – time just wouldn't pass. John Joe sat in his chair by the fire from morning until night, and he barely spoke. There was little for anyone to do except watch him and make sure he took the necessary tablets at the prescribed times.

When John Joe did speak, it was usually to ask about Nana. *Where's my matron?* It was obvious that he didn't really have a handle on how long she'd been gone. You could say that she was just at mass, and would be back in an hour, and he would believe you. He would ask again in a few minutes anyway. I usually just answered that she was visiting the doctor, that they were taking good care of her, and that she would come home as soon as she could. It didn't matter what I said.

My aunt rooted out a stack of CDs from a cupboard somewhere; scratched disks that had once been given away free with Sunday newspapers. They contained terrible recordings of classic Irish ballads and drinking songs, and John Joe would sing along happily. He sang without any care for accuracy or consistency, joining in whenever a line occurred to him, usually during the chorus, and singing at whatever pitch felt right in that moment. The layering of his voice, thin and surprisingly high, against the professional recordings – often records of live performances, complete with stage banter and audience noise – was incredibly beautiful, and oddly haunting. You could almost hear the gears working, drawing back from some unimaginable depth the muscle-memory combination of melody and lyric. Really the most remarkable thing about the songs was that he remembered them. It's hard not to imagine where and how those memories were inscribed; the dark and smoke-filled backrooms of local pubs, or the long Sunday afternoons at home with only the radio for company.

Many of the songs were about the experience of emigration. John Joe had never left the country, so his experience of emigration was, like my own, one of watching other people leave – his brothers and sisters, his children. But much of the emigrant experience, as recounted and explored in these folk songs, is simply about distance. *I would swim over / The deepest ocean / Just for nights / In Ballygrand*, go the lines in 'Carrickfergus', a song I only came to understand in that kitchen during that week. These songs were filled with people looking back at a far-off past, dreaming about old flames and long-lost landscapes.

Often the sea is literally wide, but sometimes it is more ambiguous than miles plotted on a map. Sitting in the kitchen with John Joe, I was struck by the resonance between two different experiences of exile; the emigrant and the amnesiac. As the past grew more distant and foggy in his mind, gradually disappearing over some unrecoverable horizon, the songs became more important and more accurate too. They were a link with that past, that foreign country, even as they dramatised the experience of losing it. John Joe sang like a man whose boat was filling rapidly with water. He had a very wide ocean to cross, one he could not swim over.

The CDs were old, and the stereo unreliable; every few minutes the music would skip and stutter, and then cut out completely, leaving only the descending whine of the disk on its spindle as it wound to a stop. I got more frustrated at this than John Joe did, probably because he couldn't remember all the times it had already happened. When a song did miraculously play through to its conclusion, John Joe would look at me and say, with as much heart as he could muster, *Get that man another pint!*

Nana stayed in the hospital for a week. We visited her at the weekend and she looked well. She was in the mood to reminisce, and she told us some old stories none of us had heard before. The doctors decided to keep her under supervision for a few more days. She was transferred briefly to Dublin for some tests, and my mother went with her. Apparently my gentle, sickly grandmother got a real kick out of speeding through the city traffic in the ambulance, sirens wailing.

While Nana was away, home-help arrived for the first time. You could say there was something slightly underhanded about her children waiting until her back was turned before inviting strangers into her home, but it was unquestionably the right thing to do. She was in hospital precisely because of the toll that caring for John Joe was taking on her; she had nothing left for taking care of herself. At first, the home-help consisted of an affable middle-aged man who checked in briefly in the morning to fill buckets of turf, wash dishes, and help John Joe to shave and shower. Sometimes he would drop in again on his way home, later in the afternoon. Gradually, a team of carers started to appear at set intervals throughout the day. With the exception of the first, they were all women. Right to the end, it was women who bore the brunt of his care. John Joe would sing to those kind and efficient women while they brought him to the bathroom, or changed his clothes. He'd make a great show of kissing their hands when they were leaving. They displayed no signs of irritation or impatience with him and his harmless playacting – I suppose this was the more pleasant end of what they had to deal with every day. Despite the difficulty of their jobs – despite the emotional cost, the constant travel, and the chronic underpayment – they managed to maintain an air of perpetual good cheer. They wore their responsibilities lightly, at least in front of us.

When Nana came home, it seemed like the break had done her some good. She was weak, but in great spirits. In the hospital, she had been taken care of in a way she'd hardly allow at home and, while I wouldn't say she got used to the idea, she seemed a bit more concerned with herself afterwards, which was no harm. She was nervous around the home-help at first, worried about what they thought about her, about John Joe, or about the house. When she saw how capable they were, and how sincere, she started to come around. Gradually, she became used to their visits, realising how much weight they took off her shoulders.

—

On Father's Day that year, three months after Nana returned from the hospital, my dad took John Joe for a drive into town. John Joe was in the habit then of calling the place, with its population of 1,200 people, *the deserted village*. They cruised around looking at the shops, pubs and fields. In the passenger's seat of his old jeep, John Joe got emotional in the way he often did around then. *It's great to see it all one last time*, he kept saying. *It's as if he knew he was going to die*, my father told us after.

John Joe didn't die. The following morning he went into a nursing home for a week to give Nana a break. For months, he'd been sitting by the range in the kitchen, fretting his cap about his head and repeating the same few phrases again and again. Whenever anyone came into the kitchen he would say *Nobody home*, and when they left he'd call out, *I'll see ye in church*. The repetition was driving my grandmother crazy, so when the idea of him going into the home for a week was put to her – albeit dressed up as something more palatable than it was – she was all for it. I didn't see him leave, but I know she was down to the bog almost as soon as he was gone. She didn't light a fire until after four o'clock that afternoon, an aberration that shocked everyone. As the week drew on, she spent more time in the bog, more time in her garden, more time anywhere but that kitchen. It was warm and peaceful outside and all the trees were at their fullest. The bog was busy with neighbours, and the fields were dotted with birds picking at the exposed ground after the hay had been cut. While slicing thin cuts of beef one afternoon, she told me she'd made twenty-two stucks of turf in the bog that morning. I could see the pride on her face, she was flush with it. She just hoped he'd stay gone until the turf was home.

—

In July, I woke to the sound of hooves galloping past my bedroom window, and my brother's face at the door. Our parents were away, and we were looking after the place. Some cattle had broken out of a field and were running loose around the house and garden. Neither of us were quite sure what to do with these liberated animals – we didn't know where exactly they'd come from, or where we were supposed to put them now. We'd both herded animals up and down the road since we were children, but we had never been put on the spot like this. We'd never had to make decisions without supervision.

We stood outside in the garden and fidgeted uselessly for ten minutes before our neighbour appeared and took over. During that time, John Joe stood at the front door of his house, joyously singing 'The Belle of Belfast City': *I'll tell me ma / when I go home / the boys won't leave the girls alone* ...

I can't recall where Nana was – maybe this was around the time she'd tripped over the cord of John Joe's electric blanket and hit her head against a bedside locker, sending her back to hospital for a day or two. Maybe she was at the doctor, or maybe just in town with her daughter. All I can see when I think of that morning now is John Joe, looking alive and boisterous, absolutely thrilled by the confusion outside his door. There was a time, only a couple of years before, when he would have stepped in and immediately taken charge of the situation. He would have told us exactly what to do and made sure we were doing it quickly and correctly. Instead, he stood in the doorway and called out his stock phrases to us, his tired old snatches of song. They felt like taunts – they were so ridiculous, so unbearably out of place. He was like an oblivious child at a funeral, singing his playful, happy songs like he hadn't a care in the world.

—

My memories of John Joe's declining health are all like this – episodic, indistinct, unreliable. These were discrete events separated by weeks or months when I wasn't there, and it is difficult to piece them back together in the right order, with all the relevant details intact.

Looking back on it now, I think the spaced repetition – that succession of intervals – was definitive. Each time I came home, it felt a little different – relationships were altered, intimacies were lost, the worry grew heavier. The place was steadily overcome with a sense of watchfulness; a near-constant anxiety, wary and expectant. Sometimes it was hard to tell what my parents had become used to, and what they had yet to notice.

I tried to take advantage of my distance, to pay attention to what was changing and what was staying the same. Whenever I saw or heard something interesting, I said to myself, *remember that*. Of course, if I didn't write it down – and usually I didn't – it disappeared. A lot of the time, nothing interesting happened anyway, and my hopes of retrieving meaning and significance from the situation were thwarted. I would return to Dublin with nothing to report. Now, looking for patterns and stories in the past, I feel like that time is already slipping away – where was I? What happened? What was I thinking? The lived timeline of those months – the sense of decline and inevitability; the frustration and pain of living with a terminal disease – is being replaced in my mind by static pictures. What once flowed is now frozen, and choice moments are made to stand in for a lost sense of succession.

But these frozen events are not indicative of how anything felt during those months. It was precisely time's inexorability that bore down hardest on everyone. It's not like these episodes even had any great bearing on what came after them. For every occasion that sparked some further curiosity in me – such as listening to John Joe sing while Nana was in hospital, or his morbid Father's Day drive – there were countless boring, sad, mundane days where nothing out of the ordinary happened at all, and the necessary, uninspiring labour of care and concern carried on uninterrupted. Most of the time, I had the privilege of being spared those mundane days, that exhausting effort. I wasn't living with his condition as a daily reality. I could approach each visit with a relatively brazen optimism; not for anyone's prospects of improvement, but for the opportunity I would have to notice something meaningful, or memorable. Something I could use. Unlike the women who came to provide indispensable care, unlike my father and his sisters, I got to come and go on my own schedule, and to maintain my own aims and desires. I got to pretend like I knew what was happening, or how people really felt, even when I was doing little more than mutely watching others bear the labour and responsibility of caring for my grandparents. Meanwhile, those closest to home continued with their thankless work – softening blows, salvaging what could be salvaged; and all the while showing a cheerful face to the world.

the blow-in

*How easy it is to lose sight of what is historically invisible —
as if people lived only history and nothing else.*
　—John Berger, *Our Faces, My Heart, Brief as Photos*

We drove to Boora again on St Stephen's Day, wanting to feel the wind on our faces. My brothers and I had bought my mother a new camera for Christmas, and she was itching to test it out. My father had a new watch that tracked his movement, so he was updating us regularly on his step count. When we arrived, shortly after lunch, my aunt and her partner were in the car park, just about to leave. We'd all had the same idea: get out of the damn house. It wasn't a particularly nice day, but it wasn't raining either.

We stopped periodically as my mother framed photographs: the reeds at the edge of a lake, an abandoned peat train rusting on its side, my father and I, posing on the gravel path cutting through the forest. Strangely, she never checked how the photos came out after she took them. It was only when we had almost completed our lap around the park that she noticed the camera's focus had been set to manual the entire afternoon. Every photo she'd taken, even those she'd spent several minutes getting just right, were blurred and fuzzy.

It was getting dark when we came back around to the entrance. My father decided to take the long way home. We turned down a narrow road I'd never noticed before, and the view from the back seat was as untamed as anything I'd seen in this part of the country. The boundaries between bog and farm seemed to break down entirely. Houses, sheds, and farmyards appeared out of nowhere, perched on the edge of a blankness beyond. It was as if they'd carved a little bit of calm out of the bog many years previous, and had spent all the time since being attacked and undermined by feral wilderness. Whatever civilising sense they had was porous and partial. Nothing grew straight. Every bush and tree was a mass of tangles and nothing man-made remained square for long. Fences and gates were crumbling, and the breeze block walls of tin-roofed sheds sagged into the soft ground at incongruous angles. The road itself was one long twist punctuated by jagged potholes. The leafless branches of hardy roadside trees reached out towards us, desperate and lonely. This was Turraun.

The wild stretch ended as suddenly as it had taken hold. We came around a sharp corner only to be presented with a row of completely typical country bungalows, all of them very much like our own. They had gravel drives and verdant front lawns, pools of tidy green and white set in relief against the vast, brown-yellow badlands. They were so neat and orderly, I couldn't believe it. Toys in the yard, goalposts in the garden, Christmas lights in the windows – everything was utterly normal. I wondered aloud how they had even managed to sink proper foundations for houses like these; the ground must have been shifting beneath them. Despite appearances, we were still very much in the bog, and these clean, modern houses could surely extend no more in the direction from which we'd come lest they collapse and be swallowed up entirely by the wet and twisted wilderness. Still, my mother told me that a friend of hers lived in one of these houses, and that when she had visited our house a few months before, she'd said, *God, you're really in the sticks out here.*

—

Turraun was always a wasteland, but it was also the first place in Ireland where people successfully mechanised the archaic manual labour of peat-harvesting. At the time, turf was burned in homes all across the country, and moss peat was processed for use in gardening and horticulture. If you could produce enough of it – and then transport it to the cities, where people actually bought it – you stood to make a decent amount of money. The challenge was drying it quickly and consistently; more moisture in the peat meant heavier, less-effective fuel and compost. Traditionally, peat was dried in the open air, but that took weeks and was subject to the whims of the weather. If the peat could be dried indoors, by use of an oil-fired burner, then the opportunities for speed, efficiency, and reliability were vast.

The first person to coherently apply the logic of automation and scale to that process was a local man named Farrell, who set up shop in Turraun around 1904. The only picture I've seen of Farrell shows him as an older man, thin, with a long face and sharp, knowing eyes staring into the middle distance. He had worked on the bog for years before he struck out on his own and secured the finance needed to buy machinery, build factory sheds, and hire men. However, the business was not as profitable as he'd hoped, and he got into considerable debt. The operation was soon bought out by one of Farrell's creditors, an ex-army officer named Colonel Dopping. There were several retired military men making inroads into the peat industry in Ireland at the time. Ordering around impoverished workforces, the regulation and improvement of foreign land – maybe this was the closest men like Dopping could come to replicating their experiences in the further-flung corners of the Empire. Dopping himself had been a part of the colonial administration in India, and he brought to Turraun an Indian servant who lived with him on his houseboat on the river Brosna.

I don't know anything about this servant beyond the fact of his existence, but ever since I learned of him, I've been as fascinated by his story as the locals of Turraun must have been a century ago. I imagine the servant was a man – would the alternative have been a scandal? Something about the intimacy of the houseboat and the distance they had travelled together suggests more than a simple master–servant relationship between the two men. Dopping must have relied on his servant, and trusted him.

I imagine the servant waking first and stepping across the cold boards of the houseboat as he lights the fire in the small iron stove, fills the tin kettle and leaves it to slowly boil. He does this without thinking, as he has for many years. The narrow interior of the boat is simple and bare; there is not much to do most days. Dopping emerges in shirtsleeves when the kettle begins to sing. The servant brings him breakfast. Dopping drinks his tea and, for a few minutes after eating, smokes his pipe absent-mindedly. There is no talk. Soon Dopping dresses and leaves for his concern on the bog, while the servant is left to clean away the plates and pans. He might have been confined to the boat and forced to pace its claustrophobic quarters until Dopping's return. But it's not like he was going to run away. He was hardly inconspicuous, and it was a long way home.

—

From what I can tell, this part of the world was histori-cally unwelcoming to outsiders. In Helen Sheil's account of the area in the two decades before the Famine, she tells the story of people from across the Shannon being chased out of town in case they drove up the price of potatoes. She describes how people who let strangers stay in their houses would be taken to task by gangs of local vigilantes. The reason for this suspicion and hostility was simple: there wasn't enough food, work, or land to go around. Outside of the Protestant landowners, who dictated both rents and wages, nobody had a pot to piss in. They lived in one-room hovels, pushed further and further into the bogs by rising rents and the need for more productive land use. Why have peasants on your best land when you could have much more valuable crops or animals? This is probably why my grandparents' house is where it is: the cheapest, most marginal land, reserved for the poorest, most marginal people.

Those who worked that land in the 1830s had neither the time nor the money to travel and experience other places. Sheil mentions how, from the road into the town, you can see the Slieve Bloom mountains on the horizon, twenty miles away – many people would never even have gone that far. These were people with a maddeningly limited sense of the world, a locality hemmed in tight by the forces of poverty, hard labour, and imperialism. This is one of the most painful elements of Sheil's account: the sense of interminable decline and festering neglect leading to a hard, astringent narrowness. People turning against each other, turning against the world. The title of Sheil's book: *Falling Into Wretchedness*.

A place does not cast off that kind of history lightly. Towns like ours still bristle at the sight of difference, and change comes slowly if it comes at all. The details may differ over the years, but the forms remain terrifyingly static. Sometimes it seems like everything has been inherited. The restrictions can be suffocating, the air of 'normality' noxious. This feeling was depressing to me as a teenager, and it's still confusing now. I want to live with all the comforts of tradition and familiarity, but with none of the narrowness, none of the stricture and fear. I want that to be possible, but I don't know how it could be. Exasperated and accusatory, I'm left to ask myself an unanswerable question: how could anything improve if those who want change are the first to leave?

—

Foreigners like Dopping's servant still rarely make their home around our bog, but there is nothing unusual now about people travelling from great distances to visit here. Going to school in Clonmacnois – we were taught to spell it without the 'e' – meant observing a year-round stream of tourists coming to see the monastery there, and take pictures of the ruined Norman castle. We were children and these things were just the backgrounds to our days, seen through the fog as we got off the bus in the morning, or gazed at distractedly while waiting for the lunch bell to ring. We were aware of their history, which was drilled into us in class, but these sites never felt of purely historical importance; their story, which was our own story, was still ongoing. Meeting busloads of German and American tourists wandering around was just the ordinary way of things. Sometimes they would come up to the wall of the school and talk to us. Nowadays a large fence separates the children from the visitors, hung with signs explaining that photographing kids is prohibited.

We took it for granted that all these people would travel such long distances to this quiet, cold, out-of-the-way place to see things we saw almost every day of our young lives. My mother, who has worked in the school for almost twenty years, says this idea fascinates the tourists too. They are amazed that the children grow up looking out on such a historical, picturesque landscape. But the familiar is a habit; soon it goes unnoticed, absorbed into the daily pattern of life. This is just as true for children, who have known nothing else, as it is for adults. Sometimes, as my mother parks her car in the school car park, turning at the top of the hill, she looks out over the Shannon, the morning light on the flowing surface of the river, the castle and the monastery all in ruins, and she will stop and think of how lucky she is to work in such a beautiful and unique place. But most days, she says, she doesn't notice it at all.

—

What began in Turraun at the turn of the 20th century soon became a national industry. The Turf Development Board was founded in 1933, the year my grandfather was born, with the idea of developing the bogs as a national energy resource. With coal proving scarce during the war years, turf production almost doubled by 1945. In 1946, the Turf Development Board became Bord Na Móna, transforming from a private company to a semi-state operation. The first peat-fired power station came online a decade later, and others sprang up all around the countryside. Many miles of narrow-gauge train tracks were laid down. Chugging locomotives carried peat toward tall chimneys in the distance. Men learned how to operate incredible new machinery, which they tweaked and improved based on their particular needs. Generations of experience on the bogs fed into the success of a truly indigenous concern.

For the first time, the Midlands had an industry of its own, and a need for skilled and unskilled labour. Men came from all over the country to live in temporary camps and work long days on the bog. In time, whole villages were built to house them and their families. Farmers could find seasonal work to supplement their farming income. They

could train as fitters, welders, electricians, and mechanics.
Scientists, architects, engineers, accountants – the Bord had
need of them all. For some, it was the difference between
something and nothing. For others, getting a job with
Bord Na Móna was a lifetime commitment, an opportunity
for personal growth and professional development.

I don't think John Joe had any great plans when he
joined Bord Na Móna around 1980. He probably just
needed the money. He was almost fifty, a part-time farmer
with six children aged between ten and twenty-five. There
were many more like him – ordinary people; locals.

The bogs, which for centuries had been a drain on the
capacity of local agriculture, were now one of the primary
sources of productivity for the area. People who would
undoubtedly have left home, and probably the country, in
search of work had the chance to stay and live decent lives in
their own place. The towns that grew up around the power
stations, and the communities who worked on the bog
between those towns, were able to support growing families. Those families became teachers, publicans, builders,
typists, farmers, grocers, nurses, and factory workers.

—

'The bog is not for me an emblem of memory,' writes Tim
Robinson, 'but a network of precarious traverses, of lives
swallowed up and forgotten.' This feels to me like the
most accurate and useful encapsulation of what the bog

has done and is still doing in the lives of those who live alongside it. The bog is not an endpoint at the edge of the human world, nor a stratum beneath it, but an environment shaped by the ongoing wanderings of people coming in and out of it. To traverse the bog is to beat a path through it, leaving a trail for others to follow, or following those who have gone before. Such a path is always communal; some sense made of the wilderness over time.

The mystery of the bog, and its attraction, lies in the way it both remembers and rejects the paths we make. It is, to borrow Derek Gladwin's phrase, *contentious terrain*. Contentious not just in how ambiguous its significance or its habitability may be, but because the bog sometimes appears to have a will of its own, an unpredictable and typically dark force that pushes back against the presence of human life. We walk into it, but the ground springs back behind us, immediately overgrown, as if we had never been. The bog has a life like the rest of us; it changes with us, in response to us, and has its own sense of becoming. The bog, of all things, should never been seen as fixed.

Perhaps this is why Tim Robinson adds that caveat to his description of the bog: 'lives swallowed up and forgotten'. This constant tension between preservation and obliteration – between meaning and void, presence and absence, silence and sound – this is what defines the experience of the bog. The paths we make in and out of it are always shifting and unreliable. And yet they persist, winding inscrutably through the apparent blankness, inviting yet another pilgrim to thread a way; to pass through, or to sink foundations.

—

Not long before stumbling upon Dopping's servant, I read Rebecca Solnit's *Book of Migrations*, where she describes how every place exists in two versions – exotic and local. 'The exotic is a casual acquaintance who must win hearts through charm and beauty and sites of historical interest,' she says, 'but the local is made up of the accretion of individual memory and sustenance, the maternal landscape of uneventful routine.'

The occasion for these thoughts is a trip through the Burren in Co. Clare. For Solnit, writing in the mid-1990s, the Burren was a place becoming almost exclusively exotic. Thanks in part to the waves of travellers passing through, and in part to the lack of economic opportunity for locals, the balance between individual memory and historicised importance had shifted, more or less conclusively, toward the latter. The attractions of the Burren for the transient tourist and the settling retiree were obvious: a uniquely beautiful landscape of geological and historical value; an old and yet accessible reserve of 'traditional' Irish culture; a romantic wilderness of primitive, warm-hearted survival on the edge of the continent; the thrashing ocean at the foot of the cliffs. The draw was less apparent for those who were born and raised there.

When I read that passage, sitting at my parents' kitchen table some years ago, I immediately began to think of my relationship to home in the same terms. Here, I felt, was a place becoming exotic, though in a manner quite different to the Burren. The Midlands do not have the easy appeal of the west coast. For most people, the heart of the country is a barren expanse to pass through on the way to somewhere else.

I immediately understood Solnit's 'exotic' as a large-scale, communal forgetting, and my home, it seemed to me on that winter evening, was a place in the process of being forgotten entirely. It was a place where the possibilities of life's endurance were being cut away, a place of purely historical interest. I thought of the houses all around, and I thought of the widows who lived alone in so many of them. Families had been disappearing from here time out of mind – my grandfather was, after all, the only son of five who stayed here; my father, the only son of four to do the same. I couldn't say whether I, or either of my brothers, would ever really live there again. I felt like the place was thinning out. It couldn't support the lives it needed to push on, to keep going and stave off a silent collapse. A time would no doubt come when everything that had happened here, everything we had built, all the paths we had taken, would be lost. I resolved to remember, to do the work that might, in some small way, sustain life and routine in this circumscribed locality.

Of course, this is nonsense. I mean, what would I know about what the place needs or doesn't need? My way of seeing things had little or nothing to do with the reality of the people who live there. My position, not unlike Solnit's, was that of an interested and concerned observer, sheltered from a process over which I had no influence at all. I could go to the library and read about the history of our area, but I would not live there. I could gather my notes and sketch out theories, but still I could not know what my parents and my grandparents knew. Just recently, sitting at our kitchen table while my parents and two aunts discussed various people who lived around us – their houses, their families, their histories – I was again struck dumb by the depth of their knowledge, the extensive catalogue of names and connections that was threaded through their lives. The only one who was forgetting, really, was me.

The things I had been accumulating – characters like Dopping's servant; books like *Falling Into Wretchedness*; phrases like 'network of precarious traverses' – were not a part of the lives and minds I considered local. Solnit is explicit: the exotic is history, the local is memory. Sincere and even passionate as it might be, my relationship to home had become a mostly intellectual pursuit. Writing about it was not going to reverse that. I wonder if it is even possible to write entirely from memory, or whether memory is, in the end, a private, unspoken, unspeakable thing. To put something into words at all is to manufacture a distance, a partiality, which is exotic, which turns memory into history. I take Dopping's servant out of his archival existence and I wheel him about on the stage I've set for him, and I do so because he is interesting, because he is exotic, because he is a part of history now, no matter what I do.

I make use of him because I want to believe that even someone so foreign, so other, could become a part of this locality; that he could be woven into the story of this part of the world. I want to hope that this place, these people, would admit such difference into their lives and their ideas of what is normal, and who is local. Solnit calls the idea of nativeness a 'myth of singularity', and I want to expand my own version of that myth – to believe that some poor man from the other side of the world – alone and practically imprisoned – could also have called this place 'home'.

Selfishly, I want to believe that being a local, living in the rut of 'uneventful routine', would not dull the exotic charm and beauty of a place. Because I feel like I need both. If I am to be happy, if I am to feel at home, I need both; the abstract and the concrete, the theoretical and the practical, the familiar and the unfamiliar. And I'm not sure I can have that at home, in the place where I grew up. What causes me to respond to something in a way that feels true, what binds me tighter to the people or places around me, is altogether different than what gave my parents and grandparents a similar feeling. We started out in the same place, but the courses of our lives have been so different. I have lost much of what they had, even as I gained things they never imagined. I have so many choices in life, but I have lost the ability to say: *this is the centre of the world*. Maybe this is what being local really is – the ability to say, without doubt or any subsequent clauses, *this is my home*.

machine learning

It is just by means of ordinary life and conversation, by abstaining from meditating and from studying things that exercise the imagination, that one learns to conceive the union of soul and body.

—René Descartes

John von Neumann had the biggest house in Princeton, New Jersey. It was white clapboard, two storeys, with a garage and a basement and a big garden. It was an all-American house, a postcard house. Von Neumann lived there with his second wife, Klara Dan. They hosted cocktail parties and all von Neumann's fellow professors came along with their wives. *Life* magazine said those old geniuses got *downright approachable* at the von Neumanns'. Klara Dan was a former figure-skating champion and von Neumann was her third husband. She was eight years younger than him. She was one of the world's first computer programmers. He was a genius.

Von Neumann grew up in Budapest in the years before the First World War, a smart and driven young boy from an upper-middle class family in one of the most dynamic and cosmopolitan cities in Europe. His father, Max, was a lawyer for a bank. His mother, Margit, was the daughter of a wealthy businessman who sold agricultural equipment to Hungary's booming farm industry. Von Neumann and his two brothers, Nicholas and Michael, were raised in lavish quarters on the top floor of their grandfather's building at 62 Vaczi Boulevard, a few hundred metres from the Danube. Max conducted family meals as if they were university seminars, lecturing and discussing a wide range of intellectual and political topics with his young sons. Teachers of French, Italian and English all came to the home, and they were joined in 1910 by a fencing instructor known as the Professor. Von Neumann showed no promise with the sword, and little more with the piano or the cello. Maths was his thing.

He attended the Lutheran Gymnasium in Budapest from the age of ten. Von Neumann's maths teacher, Laszlo Ratz, quickly recognised his student's ability, and arranged for his further mathematical education at the University of Budapest. By the time he was seventeen, von Neumann was seen more as a colleague than a student by the university tutors. His first academic paper was published in 1922, and it concerned 'the zeros of certain minimal polynomials and the problem of the transfinite diameter, aiming for a generalisation of Fejer's previous theorems on location of the roots of Tschebycheff polynomials'.

Von Neumann earned a degree in chemical engineering in Zurich and Berlin, while at the same time pursuing an advanced doctoral degree on the axiomatisation of Georg Cantor's set theory at the University in Budapest. He received his PhD in 1926, at the age of twenty-three.

In 1929, the year his father died, von Neumann was offered a position at Princeton and became engaged to Mariette Kovosi, a twenty-year-old from Budapest he'd known since childhood. They were married on New Year's Day, 1930, and arrived in New York by boat soon after. They were joined the following week by Eugene Wigner, a friend and former schoolmate of von Neumann's who had also been invited to Princeton. Wigner, who later won the Nobel Prize, said that von Neumann immediately took to his new home. 'Von Neumann fell in love with America on the first day,' he said. 'He thought: these are sane people who don't talk in those traditional terms which are meaningless. To a certain extent the materialism of the United States, which was greater than that of Europe, appealed to him.'

Kovosi left von Neumann for a PhD student named Horner Kuper in 1937. She called Kuper 'Desmond' because he looked like her favourite china dog of that name. Von Neumann married Klara Dan the following year.

Von Neumann lived in America for twenty-six years. During that time he published work on, amongst other things, game theory, set theory, geometry, and quantum mechanics. He was one of the first scientists to discuss the likelihood of global warming as a result of burning oil and coal. He oversaw the development of ENIAC, one of the earliest electronic general-purpose computers. He used it to test the feasibility of thermonuclear weapons. He was a major contributor to the Manhattan Project and helped to develop the atomic bombs used on Hiroshima and Nagasaki. He witnessed the first test of an atomic bomb in New Mexico and became a strong advocate for the strategy of 'mutually assured destruction' in the early years of the Cold War. He was, by his own admission, 'violently anti-communist, and much more militaristic than the norm'.

Von Neumann collaborated with Alan Turing on the philosophy of artificial intelligence when Turing visited Princeton in the 1930s. He devised the architecture that underpins almost all modern computing by keeping both information (data) and instructions (programs) in the same place. Before the discovery of DNA and long before the sequencing of the human genome, von Neumann said that living creatures contained, hardwired on the cellular level, the instructions for their own reproduction. He figured that self-reproduction could be logically and algorithmically defined, that it could be studied, worked on and improved. He thought it could be replicated with computers. He was the first person to use the term 'singularity' in relation to technology and human history – he believed, as so many do now, that computers would someday become self-aware, and that we would eventually construct a mechanical consciousness more intelligent and more powerful than ourselves. For von Neumann, it was just a matter of time before we were outstripped.

—

Shortly before his death in 1957, von Neumann began writing a lecture series, which was posthumously published as *The Computer and the Brain*. In this unfinished work he set out to define, as Ray Kurzweil writes in his foreword to the most recent edition, 'the essential equivalence of the human brain and a computer'. Von Neumann acknowledged the 'deep structural differences' between the brain and the computer, but nonetheless envisioned a strategy that would describe the brain's functionality as computation. At the heart of this idea is a conception of the human nervous system as essentially digital: the neurons in the brain either fire or they don't. One or zero.

In this view, the brain is a mixed system of analogue and digital processing – a system that was slower than computers even in 1957, but much more efficient in terms of space. Where computers tend to work, even now, in a procedural manner, the brain can do many things simultaneously. 'Large and efficient natural automata are likely to be highly parallel, while large and efficient artificial automata will tend to be less so, and rather to be serial,' is how von Neumann puts it. Though it was impossible for him to speak definitively about the complexity of trillions of neural connections, he felt the firing of a neuron was at bottom 'an essentially reproducible, unitary response to a rather wide variety of stimuli'.

It has become normal to think of creatures as running on some software we haven't yet learned to fully decode. When researchers successfully store gigantic amounts of data in a scrap of DNA or encode a video into living bacteria, when genetic modification of plants and animals is an everyday occurrence, this line of thinking appears to be logical and natural. Von Neumann was one of the first people to think like this. He saw us, and all life, running on code. 'A system of logical instructions that an automaton can carry out and which causes the automaton to perform some organised task is called a code,' he said. 'By logical orders, I mean things like nerve pulses appearing on the appropriate axons, in fact anything that induces a digital logical system, like the nervous system, to function in a reproducible, purposive manner.'

Von Neumann never mentions consciousness in *The Computer and the Brain*. He doesn't ask the kind of philosophical questions one might expect. He doesn't discuss what makes us empathic or altruistic, what allows us to recognise other people as people, or how we develop a sense of our self. As he writes at the start of the book, he was no psychologist, so maybe he felt it wasn't his place to speculate. What seems more likely is that he felt all these things to be a product of our material existence and that any computer that could be developed to operate with our mental capacity could display many (if not all) of the same characteristics of consciousness. It would just be necessary to build a computer powerful enough, and leave it free to interact with both similar computers and human beings.

At what point would we recognise such a computer as intelligent? That is the question that Alan Turing set out to answer, in a roundabout way, in 1950. Turing's idea was to formulate the question in a subtly but nonetheless radically different way. He doesn't ask: *Can machines think?* He asks: *Can a machine convince a human that it is not a machine?* This is called the Turing Test.

The test is more philosophical than it first appears. There is of course the non-trivial technical element of programming a computer able to emulate human behaviour in a given situation, and that is a practical task many have taken up in the past seventy years. The major insight of the test is the role played by recognition, and the importance of context. Turing wilfully evades the question of what we mean by 'machine' and 'think' and foregrounds our rather more immediate and intuitive recognition of thinking when we see it. The question is no longer, *What is thought?* but rather, *Does this function as thought here and now?* This is why Turing called it an 'imitation game' – it's not quite the real thing, but what does it matter when we don't know what the real thing is? As Turing himself says, 'the only way by which one could be sure that machine thinks is to be the machine and to feel oneself thinking … It may be the most logical view to hold but it makes communication of ideas difficult.'

Turing suggested that the imitation game could be satisfactorily played by a machine with a storage capacity half that of the *Encyclopaedia Britannica*, 11th edition. As the storage capacities of computers grew exponentially, many people tried stuffing them with information to see if they would start to do something like thinking. Dan Auerbach writes about one of the major efforts in this direction – the Cyc project, begun in 1984. 'A team of researchers under the direction of Douglas Lenat set about manually coding a comprehensive store of general knowledge,' Auerbach says. 'What it boiled down to was the formal representation of millions of rules, such as "Cats have four legs" and "Richard Nixon was the 37th President of the United States".' Cyc would use these rules to reach presumably logical conclusions. Cyc now contains over 5 million assertions; apparently 100 million would be required before it would be able to reason like a human.

Auerbach makes the point that computers are dumb. As Ada Lovelace said of Charles Babbage's Analytical Engine in the 1840s, 'It can do *whatever we know how to order it* to perform.' The implication is that a computer can't do anything we don't already know how to do. As the Cyc project makes clear, it's an intensely laborious task to feed information into computers. One has to proceed very intentionally, with precise, logical steps. There are so many potential pitfalls, so many unintuitive dead-ends. You really have to think the whole thing through. This becomes very difficult when you have to translate from natural language into computer language, and then teach the computer to respond in human language. Auerbach examines the logic behind the early online search engines like Yahoo, which was a manually updated index of web pages, and Ask Jeeves, which encouraged the user to ask actual questions, which it would then transform into a query it could understand. Like Cyc, Ask Jeeves used hard-coded rules to determine what the answer should be, but rather than looking within its own memory, it scanned the internet looking for instances of the query's keywords in close proximity to what looked like a plausible answer. This kind of pattern recognition might result in the right answer for simple questions, but unusual formations or atypical use of words would be confusing. Auerbach reaches the same conclusion as Lovelace: 'It only knew to look for those patterns because humans had hard-coded them.'

Google discovered a way around the problem of language and data entry. Rather than trying to understand what the user was asking and providing the correct answer, Google's algorithm searched the internet for relevant results. Google's great innovation was coming up with an algorithmic recipe to determine that relevance. 'Signals of a page's standing are determined from the topological layout of the web and from lexical analysis of the text, but *not* from semantic or ontological understanding of what the page is about,' says Auerbach. Google figured out that understanding the graph created by the way information flowed through the web was what made them valuable. They could parse the relationships, not the facts. You didn't need to understand the information, you just needed to know where it was. And every time someone searched and clicked, you could get a little bit better at understanding how it all fit together.

This 'subsymbolic' approach would surely have pleased Turing, and it has now spread well beyond the world of internet search engines. Rather than preoccupying itself with defining each and every concept it has to deal with, a subsymbolic method of artificial intelligence focuses on reacting adequately to its situation. Auerbach describes a 2012 study by Stanford and Google engineers who created a neural network that taught itself to recognise faces. A neural network at scale is basically the closest we have to von Neumann's vision of the brain and the computer as one: they combine the speed of the computer with at least some of the parallelism of the brain. They're not as complex as what we have in our heads, but their connections are based on von Neumann's old idea of how the brain works.

In designing the network, the engineers sought to mimic particular neurons in the human brain thought to be highly selective for particular object categories: hands, faces, etc. Using 1000 computers, the network assessed 10 million images taken from 10 million different Youtube videos over the course of three days and correctly identi-fied human faces with an accuracy of 80 per cent. 'Nowhere in the programming was any explicit designation made of what constituted a "face,"' says Auerbach. 'The network evolved this category on its own. It did the same for "cat faces" and "human bodies" with similar success rates.'

The study is so impressive because defining a 'face' is no easy task for a human. The study's report asks whether a baby recognises a face because it is rewarded in some way for doing so, or simply because it sees enough of them to eventually understand what they are. This is an open question. The truth is we don't know how we recognise faces, we don't know where in the brain the concept of 'face' is stored, and we can't model that information. We just know that there are faces. We know what one looks like, but describing the definitive characteristics of a face in general is basically impossible. We know one when we see it, and we know whether it is a human face or a cat face or a rock face. We can't explain that knowledge to a computer because, like so much in our lives, we can't explain it to ourselves. What the study suggests is that the explanation might not be necessary. Perhaps there is no place in the brain where thought happens, no place where consciousness is kept. Consciousness might not be distinct from being at all – not an accumulation of anything, not a threshold we pass over at some early point in life. Maybe it is, to borrow Jean-Paul Sartre's term, *translucent*.

—

John von Neumann had an incredible memory. He seemed to rarely forget anything he considered worth remembering. Once asked to recount the beginning of *A Tale of Two Cities*, he recited the book from memory for over ten minutes, until asked to stop. He hadn't read it in fifteen years. As a parlour trick, he could read a phone book once and then tell you the names and numbers on whatever page you asked for. When he calculated the memory capacity of the brain, he did so with the assumption that the brain never really forgets anything. He was also able to accurately perform extremely complex mathematical equations at astonishing speed. At the age of six, he could divide two eight-digit numbers in his head, though he never felt himself a match for his grandfather when it came to those kinds of calculations.

At the same time, von Neumann wasn't great with names or faces. This apparently embarrassed him. He had a head for logical deduction but he wasn't great with people. Von Neumann's brain was in some ways as close to a computer as it gets. If you had a mind like that, perhaps equating the two wouldn't be so difficult. Perhaps it wouldn't even be strange.

In a delightfully non-computational use of metaphor, the neuroscientist Suzanne Corkin compares the act of remembering to cooking a stew. First you have to go to the shop and find the ingredients, then you have to put them all together in the right order and the right amounts, and then you have to cook them at the right temperature for the right amount of time – only then can you can get a satisfactory result. Whenever we remember something – an event, an emotion, a name even – we are recreating that memory, drawing the elements together in a slightly different way each time. This is how our memories shift over the years, with the composition and detail of older memories changing so slowly we don't even notice it happening. This is how we build the narratives of our lives – by selectively forgetting, by fudging the details, by dwelling within a messy, subjective, unpredictable preserve of unconsciously curated memory. It is in this way that our memories differ most profoundly from those of computers.

This is also how computers earned our trust. Humans have been outsourcing their memories for thousands of years, and people have been complaining about the dele-terious effect this has had on traditional memory since at least the time of Plato. Today we rely on computers to do a great deal of our remembering for us, and they are typically excellent at it. They're far more accurate and reliable than most of us can ever be. From quick Google searches to predictive text to the vast archives of personal history contained within email inboxes and social media databases, there is no shortage of ourselves stored off-site.

Some of this off-body memory is private and meant for personal use only, but a significant amount of it is public. With the public storage of memories comes the tailoring of memories for public display – what to keep, what to discard, what to share and where to share it. Unlike organic memory, this is an entirely conscious process that works from an ideal of how a person wants to be seen *right now*. We attempt to invest the present instant with the significance and meaning of an event that deserves to be remembered, so we give it a certain shape, a certain filter and character, which signifies the desired weight of presence, the imagined durability of the already-past. In this situation, the brain and the computer have very different priorities when choosing to save or discard an object of experience.

The traces we leave of ourselves on digital networks are regularly regurgitated to remind us of previous events and memorable occasions – presumably encouraging us to share the memory with others. But then, these are not memories in anything like the traditional sense. These snippets of our lives are not partial in the same way as our episodic memories. They're partial in that they are designed to fit the system that holds and displays them – systems that, as Molly Sauter writes, 'prod us algorithmically to create specific kinds of digital memory objects, those that are algorithmically recognizable and categorizable, as part of their functionality'. These kinds of calculated provocations are alien to our natural process of creating personal narratives. In a strange way, even though they are made by us and of us, there is no room in them for us. We can make nothing of them. These would-be mementos are static, finished, sealed off. 'We are giving up the work of remembering ourselves,' Sauter says, 'for the convenience of being reminded.'

—

Almost all press coverage of Alzheimer's disease includes key statistics on the number of people who currently suffer with it, the much-higher number who will suffer by the year 2050, and the projected costs for the treatment of all these millions of future-demented. These numbers are meant to be terrifying. They are meant to strike a sense of urgency into the reader, who is presumably already worried, either for their own sake or for a friend or family member. Why would you read the news about Alzheimer's if you weren't worried about it?

As awareness and experience of the disease has grown, the role it plays in society has changed. The vaguely pathetic but mostly accepted idea of senility has been supplanted by a universally abhorred vision of alien disease, trailing a tragic and irrevocable decline and the eventual erasure of everything we once thought ourselves to be. What's more, it is not a disease that allows for the usual war-soaked metaphors of modern illness. Where there is a ready-made language for a patient's 'fight against cancer', there is no fighting Alzheimer's. You might battle with it, but such conflict is little more than a struggle for an honourable defeat. The outcome is given.

Neither is Alzheimer's seen to invade in the same way as a cancer, or a viral disease. It is not airborne, and it is not in the water. It is not a contagious disease and lacks many (if not all) of the moral judgements that often accompany infections of that sort. The company one keeps has nothing much to do with getting Alzheimer's, and the disease is generally ignorant of things like class, race and gender. If you live long enough, you stand a good chance of getting it. It rises up from within. There's nothing you can do about it.

'A disease of the lungs is, metaphorically, a disease of the soul,' wrote Susan Sontag in her book, *Illness As Metaphor*. 'Cancer, as a disease that can strike anywhere, is a disease of the body.' Alzheimer's is a more prototypically modern ailment than either TB (the disease of the lungs) or cancer because it concerns an area that is neither spiritual nor physical, and yet encapsulates and supervenes them both in the eyes of many people: Alzheimer's is a disease of the mind.

Can Alzheimer's disease be strictly classified as either a mental illness or a physical issue? Few other physical diseases can claim such a dramatic effect on the mental world of the afflicted. When their ability to remember has sufficiently degraded, it becomes normal to hear an Alzheimer's patient described as 'no longer themselves'. On the level of identity, they are seemingly lost, gone, evacuated. And yet the pathological proof of Alzheimer's manifests itself in a distinctly physical way: beta amyloid plaques and neurofibrillary tangles in the brain. The neurons stop firing, their signals weaken until they can no longer reach out to each other, no longer connect. All of the ongoing attempts to cure or prevent Alzheimer's disease are focused on these biological phenomena. If the growth of these plaques and tangles could be arrested, there would be some hope for stalling, or possibly even repairing, the cognitive deterioration of the patient.

Perhaps it would be best to say Alzheimer's disease is an existential illness. Alzheimer's is certainly one of the most widely feared diseases of our time, not just because of the ageing population that guarantees its spread, nor even because of its currently terminal, incurable nature. Alzheimer's is feared because it attacks fundamental notions of personhood and identity. The loss of memory typically associated with Alzheimer's, combined with the disengagement from the social world, which inevitably follows memory loss, is a challenge to common understanding of how the self is formed. If, as many people believe, we are the sum of our memories, at what point does the loss of those memories result in the loss of the subject constituted by them? At a time when the dominant metaphorical logic of both the individual and society is technological, network-based, and deeply individualistic, Alzheimer's forces us to think in a different way about the lexical and social organisation of human life.

Sontag writes that multi-determined diseases are by their nature mysterious. Because their origins are foggy and their treatment uncertain, mysterious diseases are vulnerable to the wildest interpretations, the most unhinged metaphors, and the most variously effective elixirs. (Even now, a surprising amount of credence is given to those who claim to have eaten their way to a cancer cure, an idea Sontag had dismissed out of hand forty years ago.) The causes of Alzheimer's are essentially as unknown as its cure, and the typical medical advice for those worried about getting Alzheimer's is laughably general: exercise, eat well, 'keep your brain active'. Do a crossword, go for a run. This lack of understanding leads to all sorts of claims regarding possibly helpful or harmful behaviour – alcohol is bad, but maybe a little alcohol is better than none at all; being bilingual might help, while bad food or poor quality sleep might make matters worse. Stress is not good. Worms, B vitamins, fasting, statins, and arctic squirrels might all hold the key that could unlock the disease. Potentially miraculous new treatments are announced with some regularity, as are their subsequent failures in clinical trials.

Illness as Metaphor is a book dedicated to examining how the ways in which people speak about disease reflect their thinking about what a person should or should not be. This is easily extrapolated into a vision of what social life should be or should not be – their fears and hopes for their society, their nation, or any community of which they consider themselves a part. 'Modern disease metaphors specify an ideal of society's well-being analogised to physical health, that is as frequently anti-political as it is a call for a new world order,' Sontag writes. This point is crucial because it hits on how the responsibility for illness has largely been heaped on the sick individual, rather than a sick society. The metaphors of illness are anti-political because they don't suggest a need for change on a social or structural level. The mystification that surrounded cancer at the time of Sontag's writing led to a widely held suspicion that cancer was the result of various behaviours on the part of the patient. Cancer was seen, she says, as a disease of middle-class life: a disease of emotional repression affecting people who have lived rich, comfortable, accumulative lives; a disease that turned the patient from a dynamic, desiring subject into a hardened, dulled, wasted creature. The fear was that a life too focused on material wealth would result in a deadening of the spirit, a hollowing-out of emotional appetite, manifested through a malignant invasion and subsequent degeneration of the body. 'The overnourished, unable to eat,' is how Sontag puts it.

The implication of this way of thinking is not that society should be altered in some dramatic way in order to decrease the importance of financial gain and elevate the sort of spiritual and emotional freedom that would presumably reduce cancer rates. It is assumed instead that the individual patient has maladjusted in some way to the demands of modern life. They've been too greedy, too shallow, too mechanic; they've not expressed their inner feelings in a healthy way. They have not been able to find a balance in their lives, and now they're paying the price. The vision of society this cancer fantasy depicts is one where the sensible accumulation of material wealth is paramount. The regulation of what is sensible is left to the individual. The fear of cancer is, for Sontag, a fear of a capitalist society that has gone too far, a society of insane, industrialised acquisition that has been rejected forcefully by the laws and balances of the natural world.

Today's ideal of society's well-being is something like a perfectly efficient network of discrete actors working to realise their material goals. These discrete actors are to be connected to others, but never reliant on them. They must be independent, single-minded; entrepreneurial if possible but diligent if not. Empathy is to be encouraged but you don't want to be taken for a fool. Don't get too involved. Communities are built purely on aligned self-interest: professional development, property values, ideological purity. The goal is to be a useful and valuable member of a network, someone through whom information flows and is amplified. To join a network is to gain access to the information already flowing through it. The dominance of the networked computer system as a way of thinking about the world has encouraged a self-consciousness that is intimately tied up with the ability of our minds to process data, understand visual cues, recognise patterns, and interface with other minds. The more capably we do these things, the more rewarded we are likely to be in life. We will be rewarded not just with money, but with something generally more sought after: recognition.

It is in this vision of a healthy society that Alzheimer's appears as the most existentially terrifying illness one can imagine. The primary effect of Alzheimer's is to make a person utterly useless to their networks. If our identity is increasingly wrapped up in our ability to be useful in a networked context, then the fear of being a bottleneck or a burden is likely to increase. There is an indignity in no longer being able to participate in the activities of the network; a frustration at our ineptitude, our slowness, our mechanical failure. In a networked world where the distinctions between person, brain and computer have all broken down, the Alzheimer's patient is a computer that can no longer process information; a brain that can no longer follow instructions or recognise patterns; a person who has no value at all. Their relationships with the others in their network are brutally restricted, and eventually those other computer-brains will cease to recognise the broken one in their midst. It won't be worth the effort to communicate – they'll route the information elsewhere. In a world where recognition is the very material of life, to be denied it is to suffer a very painful existence indeed. It is a disintegration of personhood. It is a type of death. This process of withdrawal is not something that happens overnight, and it is the drawn-out nature of Alzheimer's that sparks some of the strongest fear. It's a fear of prolonged humiliation. The patient is, in some deeply abhorrent way, out of control. When the possibility of memory storage disappears, with it goes the ability to either interpret or communicate any information received. In the eyes of others, they may become irrational beings who can no longer follow the same logical steps as everyone else.

When there is a tremendous pressure to display for others the good and authentic life you are living, there is a subsequent fear of being seen as the tragic case who cannot exert control, who cannot recognise the patterns and codes of daily life that lead to self-improvement, ladder-climbing, material reward. The Alzheimer's patient cannot bring the past to bear on the present, and so there is no going forward. If the point of a network is that it is always growing, a node with dementia stalls that growth. The Alzheimer's patient is no longer making or sharing memories, rather they appear to be undergoing a hollowing-out. They are becoming unspecific.

The most revered people in our society today are those who seem to be in control of the way information flows. It is those people who appear to have a unique insight into the nature of the network as a whole, a perspective those of us who simply live in darkened, inconsequential corners of their networks cannot begin to imagine. Their attraction lies in the idea that they have retained an independence and power that we have largely lost. We note how the people in charge of social media networks don't actually use or trust those same networks. We envy them for this.

An Alzheimer's patient is entirely the opposite of these people. They can oversee nothing, make sense of nothing, shape nothing. They are powerless to stop the connections outside their brain shrivelling even quicker than those inside it. People who control the flow of information have always been in a position of power, but today the integral nature of information networks to work, to finance, and to social life, makes the conditions of life outside of the network ever more straitened.

The solution could be to ensure everyone uses the networks. If all communication happened through the network, a kind of total knowledge would be possible, allowing for an essentially invisible, automated, instantaneous policing of that communication. Bad actors could be removed, while valuable contributors could be rewarded. The publication of Facebook's internal guidelines for the recognition of offensive content – which used a basic version of set theory to designate 'white men' a protected category, but not 'black children' – only showed the difficulties inherent in this kind of thinking: all the logical assertions and semantic rules in the world will not add up to a living picture of language. Connecting people is easy, but understanding the implications of what they say to each other is as hard as it gets.

—

The Scottish anthropologist Tim Ingold makes the distinction between a 'network' – such as the internet – and what he calls a 'meshwork' – such as a spider's web. A network is a set of interconnected points, while a meshwork is a set of lines without terminal connections. The spider's web is a meshwork because it is the lines themselves that are important. The lines of a network, in contrast, are meaningless without their terminals. For the spider, the lines of the web are the lines along which it lives, and guide its perception and action in the world. When a fly gets caught in the web, two distinct lines of life become entangled. At the same time, the web's lines do not link or connect the spider and the fly – nothing flows between them. The lines of the web are simply the lines along which an interaction – a knotting – can take place. The lifeline of the spider and the lifeline of the fly are still unfolding in time, still open to the future, still trailing a past. The focus, if we are interested in life, is following those lines.

Ingold describes us living beings as *parliaments of lines*. He sees all life forms as a place where many ongoing lines coincide, or correspond. Life is that which gets tangled up in other lives, which knots, overflows and leaks. People, animals, trees and plants are 'forever discharging through the surfaces that form temporarily around them'. Ingold applies this 'leaking' to the idea of the mind, that strange mix of thing and no-thing. He quotes the American anthropologist A. Irving Hallowell, who argued in the 1950s that 'any inner-outer dichotomy, with the human skin as boundary, is psychologically irrelevant'. We are leaking out into the world, just as the world leaks into us. Not along the routes of networks, but along the unpredictable, open-ended lines of meshworks. Our lives are not points on a graph connected to other points that are connected to other points on other graphs. Whether the brain is a computer or not, we are not simply terminals through which information flows – we are the flowing itself. Our life, our consciousness is not some inherent arrangement of neurons in the brain. It is something that comes from the world outside the brain. The mind is a product of recognition, a product of interaction not between two discrete points on a network but a multitude of intuitive, reactive, creative lines all following their own improvised path. The mind is not confined to a particular portion of the brain, or even to the skull – it leaks out.

Those who have most fervently understood the brain to be a computer typically have little to say about a leaky mind. They see the brain as the ultimate locus of consciousness, separate in a fundamental way from both the body it controls and the world with which it interacts. For them, the difference between us and other creatures is that our brain is big and smart enough to hold itself above the world, to see the world from the point of a more-or-less disinterested observer. This vision suggests, in Ingold's words, an 'imagined separation between the perceiver and the world, such that that the perceiver has to reconstruct the world, in the mind, prior to any meaningful engagement with it'.

I guess it's possible that we do walk around as discrete and self-contained beings constantly comparing what we sense and observe with the model of the world we have in our heads. This might be how we learn the logic of the networks we live in, how information flows, and how to advantageously model ourselves within those networks. For a networked life, the passing of data between terminals is paramount. The ability to retain, analyse and repeat that data is the key to being recognised as valuable. If something obstructs those processes – something like the growth of beta amyloid plaques in the brain – then one's value disappears. One cannot recognise, and will not be recognised in turn. If someone's model of the world is so temporary, so partial, so full of holes that it barely even includes a model of themselves, then can we really say that they are conscious?

A network is a logically reduced sketch of the world. Everything is stripped back to the most efficient version of itself. Someone with Alzheimer's will, however, become about as inefficient as a person can be. Eventually nothing that passes through them will make sense to anyone else. Their brains will no longer do the kinds of things that make us think that brains are computers: they won't remember what people tell them; they won't recognise so many patterns; they won't be able to multiply and divide. Their ability to interact with others, what we might call their agency, will gradually disappear. They will become slow. Perhaps they will make a great many mistakes; perhaps they will no longer originate anything; perhaps they will no longer know how to do anything we have not told them, in very careful and logical steps, how to do. Maybe they would fail a Turing Test.

But, as Turing said, so what? A person's ability to play the imitation game is no more important to their continuing personhood than a computer's ability is to its own identity as a computer. The Turing Test is about recognition: it asks the players to recognise each other, to accept their limitations and give them the benefit of the doubt based on the circumstances in which they find themselves. The self is not trapped up there in the disintegrating brain; it relies on others to continue recognising it in the world, to continue treating it as something open-ended, to continue caring for it. The only way to know for sure that another person has stopped thinking is to be that person. The best we can do is to take them as we find them.

—

Von Neumann didn't live long enough to get Alzheimer's disease. He died at the age of fifty-three, from cancer. It was his body that let him down in the end, never his head. He spent his last few months at the Walter Reed Army Medical Center in Washington DC under military supervision lest he reveal confidential information while on heavy medication. He had been a military consultant for over fifteen years before becoming one of the most trusted advisors and committee chairmen of the Eisenhower administration.

That government made sure he took whatever secrets he possessed to the grave. During the long hospital days of winter 1956 he would recite to his brother, word-for-word from distant memory, the first few lines of each page of Goethe's *Faust*.

Though he was a lifelong agnostic, von Neumann received the last rites from a Roman Catholic priest, Father Anselm Strittmatter. This deathbed conversion was rooted more in the science of hedged bets than the ecstasy of religious conviction and it makes me think he must have considered it at least possible that he had been catastrophically incorrect about basically everything. He said to his mother in earlier years that the existence of God would make many things much easier to explain, but unlike his compatriot in the Manhattan project, J. Robert Oppenheimer, he was not much given to the use of religious metaphor. No mystical Sanskrit quotes escaped his lips as the fire of the first atomic bomb burned in the sky south of Socorro, New Mexico. He would never have called that test 'Trinity'.

Before the final sacrament was performed, von Neumann noted that, regarding his famous wager, Pascal may have had a point. Fr Strittmatter said that this concluding ritual brought little or no peace to von Neumann in his final hours. He remained terrified of death.

this is how it was

When he saw this portrait, in which he had chosen every-thing for himself, he said with a kind of relief: 'And now my great grandchildren will know what sort of man I was.'
—Jean Mohr, *Another Way of Telling*

At Christmas, I gathered all the photo albums from my grandmother's house and I carried them back up the garden to my bedroom. Then, at my mother's insistence, I climbed into our attic and collected all of our own family photographs too. Disorganised and floating loose, they filled a couple of small, battered suitcases to overflowing. I hadn't intended to look at our photographs; I wanted to see my grandparents when they were young, when they weren't grandparents, or even parents. There are few photos of their early childhood days, because cameras were not common in the homes of poor farmers in the 1930s. There is, however, a photocopy of a photograph taken in 1947 in which Nana is pictured, aged nine, as a cast member in an amateur production of *The Pearl and the Fisherman* at the local parish hall. It was her first and last appearance on stage, and she was dressed as an angel. She and her sister – also playing an angel – have their heads circled in blue ballpoint pen. The photocopy has the words 'Photographic Memories' hand-written in over-sized bubble lettering at the top of the page.

These early photographs of Nana are exciting and mysterious to me, more so than the handful that record John Joe's youth. John Joe looks stiff and uncomfortable in his early portraits, but Nana looks more alive in hers, a little mischievous sometimes; somehow more immediate, or present, even when the photo is clearly and carefully posed. She retained this quality even after her children were born, when the photographs began to appear in colour, and started to document less formal situations.

There is a particular photo of Nana that I love, or rather three photos. Two inches square, with thin white borders inside their gently serrated edges, they are pasted in a row along the top of a single page in one of her albums, like a triptych. They appear to have been taken within minutes of each other. The light in these photographs is very strong, and it looks to me like early afternoon. The brighter parts are blown out, causing the leaves on the trees in the background to turn vapourish, and to disappear. The sky is a once-brilliant white, the colour of the aged paper. Nana has short, tidy hair and she is wearing a simple polka dot dress with a white band around her waist.

The photographs are all taken from the middle of an unpaved country road, with the front windows of an unremarkable cottage visible on the left and a tall ditch receding into the distance on the right. The road is straight and draws the eye to a central vanishing point, where the subjects are placed. In the first, Nana is standing next to a seated man I take to be her brother. She has her right arm straight down by her side, and her left hand is holding the man's right. He is older than her. What remains of his hair is a little wild, and he is wearing a standard-issue suit and tie. They are both looking directly into the camera and smiling faintly.

Before I looked at it closely, I thought the second photo showed Nana sitting, hands clasped between her legs, on the knee of the same man. But it is a different man, a younger man, with darker hair and a strong, handsome face. I think this is a second brother. The fingers of his left hand are extending across his lap to brush against her hip. Nana has one foot on the ground, and her head is tilted a little, softening her pose. They both look more relaxed here than in the first photo, almost insolent. They look like they're having fun now.

The final photo is Nana alone and upright, her hands once again by her side. This photo is taken from a few feet closer to her, and she fills the centre of the frame more distinctly. The change in position has altered the light, and the shadows in the background are darker. The sunlight catches and blurs Nana's left shoulder. She looks happy, though a little nervous too, unused to being pictured alone like this. She is gazing less at the lens and more at the person behind it. That same faint smile is back on her lips. She is young here, no more than twenty-one I'd say, probably not even married yet. She is, in a manner that is rare in photographs of her, the centre of attention. Whoever took the photo wanted to remember her like that.

Another photograph in the same album, of similar style and size, shows Nana once again standing at the right shoulder of a seated man. The man now is John Joe, and he is holding aloft their first child, my uncle. They are pictured in front of his father's house, which would soon become their own. Nana's hair is longer here, not so tidy, and her hands are behind her back. She looks reticent, almost embarrassed – maybe she's just tired. She seems much older here, though only a couple of years have passed. John Joe looks tall and thin, with his legs crossed in wide trousers, and strong black shoes on his feet. He looks proud, and still a little awkward. The baby in his arms is smiling, his tiny white socks pawing against his father's hip.

—

After I had finished looking at my grandmother's photos, I began going through my mother's collection. There were many more photos here, and they were much less likely to be posed. Mostly they were amateur snaps of social events like weddings, birthdays, holidays, and nights out. There were just a couple of my mother as a child, so it was only when she and her siblings began to move away and get married, starting in the late 1980s, that the photos began to capture a sense of their lives. In one way, the sheer volume of photos my parents kept from their early years together speaks to how things were back then: they attended over a dozen weddings in the year they were themselves married. They were both twenty-three, as were most of their newlywed friends. The photographs show rural hotel function rooms, and the dance-floors of country pubs; tables laden with empty bottles and half-full glasses. My dad's head of bushy hair, his over-sized wireframe glasses; my mother, strikingly beautiful – smiling, smoking.

Gradually, these photographs give way to something more domestic. There are more images of just the two of them together, images of our house as it was being built. The gangs of friends are replaced by family, the function rooms and dance-floors by living rooms and kitchens. I show up, and then my brothers follow. We brought with us school photos, birthday cake tableaux, sandcastles, acne. Once we started appearing, I began to lose interest. I was drawn back instead to those earlier photographs, to the images that captured my mother and father in the years just before they became parents.

As I combed through these photographs, I became aware of something I'd never seen in them before. I thought,

They are so young. I looked at my soon-to-be-parents' faces and I saw, for the first time, how innocent they seemed, how green. I realised I had lived through that age myself. I had experienced that flush of wild, unchecked energy you sometimes get as a young person out in the world for the first time, when you feel like things are happening to you and for you. That spirit was evident in their faces, and I recognised it as something now in my own past. And yet the tangible products of their youthful spark – a marriage, a home, children – were still in my future, or so I hoped. I had possessed that same spark once, but I felt I had lost it, or it had simply been worn away, and I didn't even have photographs to show for it.

I looked again and again at the photographs of my parents together – so clearly *together* – as they talked and kissed in pubs, smiled triumphantly in their confetti-strewn wedding car, and embraced in the doorway of their half-built home. I was overwhelmed by love – love for them and their open, shining faces; love for the life from which these moments had come. And I felt some despair too, knowing that I would never have quite the same experience. I guess everyone feels this at some point – it is not novel, the dire certainty that you will never be young again and that you are living the only life you are going to get. It was just that they had been so young then, making the biggest decisions of their lives. By contrast, I had procrastinated endlessly and given myself a fatal amount of time to overthink. I had consistently backed away from the kind of sound choices that would have allowed me to build that kind of solid, long-term, dependable life for myself. Looking at these photographs, knowing the future they foretold, I asked myself – what could be more ambitious than this? What could be more optimistic, or more meaningful?

I had asked myself these questions before, but on that fast-darkening afternoon at the close of yet another year, something had definitely shifted in how seriously I was taking them. I was getting older. I was in a relationship that I was confident would last. In the back of my mind, I had begun to work towards ticking the boxes of what I felt a person needed to do in order to be considered mature – focusing on my career, learning to drive, opening a savings account, paying attention to mortgage interest rates. I wanted sincerely to overcome the precariousness of my life up to that point. And yet I felt restless too. The adult prospects of self-sacrifice, stability, and security were clashing with a lingering adolescent desire to wander, to throw off all responsibility and pursue the gratification of the senses like some tragic belated caricature of an itinerant artist. I knew I was too chicken to really self-destruct, so the most worrying thing was that I no longer felt, as I had for many years, that I had time and energy to do everything. Instead, I was certain there were many things in this world I would never now experience, whether I wanted to or not. Time was short, and I was already tired.

Looking at my parents in those early photographs, I was jealous not just of the choices they'd made, but that they had made them before they had time to question any of it. They hadn't, as far as I could tell, tortured themselves. They hadn't deluded themselves. They basically just did what was expected – what everyone else was doing – and it had made them happy, or happy enough at least. Even though I knew there were times when they questioned everything they'd done, I couldn't but envy them that underlying contentment. I looked at my mother's beaming, exhausted face in the newly built kitchen of our home – just across the hall from where I now sat – and felt I knew exactly what happened next. Thirty years had passed since the photograph was taken. It wasn't a bad life.

This is the joy and the pain of family photographs like these: we know what comes next. John Berger wrote that 'an instant photographed can only acquire meaning insofar as the viewer can read into it a duration extending beyond itself. When we find a photograph meaningful, we are lending it a past and a future.' The frozen instant evokes a stretch of time, a chronology, which comes alive in us. Berger talks about the 'shock of discontinuity' in such photographs, the sense that we are looking at a time that once flowed at its own particular pace, but which is now solid, arrested, motionless. It is the shock of the photograph's stubborn refusal to move, to speak, which forces the mind into action. It pushes the imagination to seek beyond the moment captured, to link the time of the photograph with our own; to recover it. The photograph gives us so much to work with – gives us, *by a precious miracle, a reality from which we are sheltered*, as Barthes puts it – and yet it cannot give us movement, cannot become animated, durational, spirited. It gives us evidence of life, not the illusion of it, and evidence is there to be pieced together, to posit something outside itself – a pattern, a story.

Because we typically know the story they depict, family photographs can make the future seem pre-ordained – as if everyone pictured knows as well as we do what is about to happen. As if it was all just destiny. This is often joyous, because fate tends towards both cruelty and kindness by turns, and we tend towards survival in either case. Knowing what the future holds, we can look back on these images and think of what was overcome in the meantime. But it can be painful too – not just because of what could not be overcome, or what did not survive, but because we cannot know the future for ourselves, and compared to these characters before us, we are clueless and lost.

—

I have always been more comfortable recording someone than taking their photo. To record someone's voice, with or without permission, doesn't really feel like stealing – it doesn't feel like I'm taking anything from anyone, or putting anyone in a compromising position. If they know I'm doing it, I feel like they don't act all that different, and neither do I. But when I have a camera in my hand, I get anxious, even more anxious than the people I'm trying to photograph. Everyone is on edge, and I can't put anybody at ease. I feel very much like an intruder then, no matter how familiar the situation. I feel like I'm not really there, that I'm already halfway out the door, making good my escape, thinking of tomorrow.

My awkwardness has meant that I have not made many photographs of my family. I did, however, take a photograph of John Joe on his second-to-last Christmas Day. He was sitting in his chair by the fire in their kitchen, and I was sitting across from him, by the door. When I lifted the camera to my eye, he looked directly at me. Looking at that photograph now, I can see he isn't smiling exactly, but he looks happy. His white hair is wet and combed, and it sticks up at the back of his head regardless. He is clean-shaven, but his skin is rough. His hands are together in his lap and his walking stick is propped against the wall behind him. You can make out the corner of a serving tray – a Christmas gift from some previous year – stuffed down behind the chair.

Most of the photos of John Joe's final years capture him in this chair, in this corner of the room. Often his children and grandchildren are arrayed around him, and Nana is by his side. In Nana's collection, I found a photo of him from before my time, sitting in the same spot, a similar half-smile on his face, watching someone take a photo of his sister-in-law and her husband. I think the intense association that developed between him and that corner of that room, combined with the placid look on his face – somewhat cheerful, almost vulnerable – produced one of the few photos of him that could reasonably be called a portrait. Nana has a copy of this photograph on the dresser in her kitchen now, and there is another in my parents' sitting room. Several of my aunts and grand-aunts have their own copies also.

The photograph was not taken with any great intent, but I got lucky – he looks himself in it. This is not a photo-graph in which one reads much of a future; I look at it and I think instead of the accumulation of life that coheres in the image of his body, the way the past is written into his presence there. The warmth and happiness I feel when looking at it comes not from what I know happens next, but from everything that took place before, the things I know and the secrets I don't; everything that led to this exact fraction of a second when an old man looked across the room at his grandson. It was rewarding to know that others have recognised John Joe in this photo, as I had, and that this moment, which I had taken and saved for myself, would serve as a way for them to keep him in their minds, to find him again when they needed him.

a deathly thing

Death is never a single end, but a collection of termina-
tions ordinarily bound so tightly together in time that they
coalesce, as single and colourless as light, into a unified
experience. Alzheimer's disease undoes that unity by
extending death, by drawing it backwards into life from
its final closure. This dying process may take several years
to reach its conclusion and, in this time, we can observe
death's interlocking components and follow its immaculate, pitiless logic.

What if I said death was the removal of a person from
the flow of time? Then we might see how a death is never
just one death, but many. A person stalls in death, and the
rest of the world flows past them, leaving them behind.
The ability of the living to go on separates us from the dead,

and the dying too, who go on so much more slowly than the rest of us. The dying, or those who are aware of it at least, get to watch the world slipping away from them, to feel themselves being left behind as one by one the people they know desert them. Not out of cruelty, not out of ignorance, but out of pure necessity – to live at death's pace is itself a kind of death, and nothing but the most sincere concern for another can sustain the living through it.

A person who dies suddenly – in an accident, or in their sleep – is lost first to themselves, and then to those who knew them best, the first to be notified. From there the word will spread, and they are lost more or less quickly to everyone who knew them. Their death echoes outward from a single point. The dying are lost over and over again, in the opposite direction. First to the world of acquaintances, colleagues, peers, who may or may not notice that they're no longer around; then to friends, distant and then close; then to family, distant and then close; and finally to themselves. And each time it is a death, each time it is the removal of a particular person from a particular flow of time. The order of one's disappearance may vary, but each time the conclusion is the same. The dying collapse inward.

—

For an Alzheimer's patient, the traditional difficulties and indignities of age are accelerated. They may, like anyone else, suffer a minor stroke or develop arthritis. They may no longer be able to drive, or to eat certain foods, or to climb to an upstairs bedroom. Their friends may die, or become otherwise incapacitated, leaving them isolated, bored, or lonely. In time, the slow extinguishing of memory unscrews the connections between brain, body and world. They no longer know the people closest to them. They feel embarrassed by their lapses. They need help dressing and undressing. They retreat.

Lying in bed on the threshold of death, the core instruments of the body – heart, lungs, demented brain – struggle on even as everything surrounding those vital forces ceases to function. The extremities are unconsciously neglected, and the warmth of life leaves them. Cold feet twitch. Eyes close. Fluids accumulate in the throat as the level of oxygen flowing through the body drops. After some time – a day, several days at most – the breathing stops and, a few minutes later, so does the heart. The living cells still left in the brain are smothered, starved, and their innumerable connections lapse, and the possibility of life is dissolved.

—

Life lived in the company of someone with Alzheimer's is life shot through with death, as if life were the shutters on a window, and death the light leaking through. Those nearest the light – friends, carers, family – are models of patience; reduced to passing the time within the walls of a ruin, waiting for the day when, as if by its own power, the light finally breaks through. They prepare for an ending that may be, for them, a new beginning – an ending that makes a mockery of desire, of progress, of clean breaks. Closure is waited upon, but it is not, except in the most desperate moments, hoped for; the end may be the best thing that can happen now, but experience tells us that not so long ago even the most ordinary and unremarkable existence was infinitely better than this.

Watching the end unfold, living with it as you prepare for it, alienation and intimacy exist in an unpredictable counterpoint; love and apathy, fear and joy, pride and regret – each woven into a single pattern. Life and death are no longer distinct territories, and the division we may have imagined between them is revealed as an illusion. Lines we may once have understood as borders separating emotions and mental states as clearly as nations on a map are seen instead as lines of action, of becoming; we pass with them through every conceivable station between sense and its opposite. We become – like the edges of a shadow, or a distant horizon – soft, blurred, and sometimes broken.

—

The experience of Alzheimer's is first and foremost a loss of temporal familiarity. It is the fatal disruption of an internal cohesion which we normally take for granted.

Our sense of ourselves as a person in the world is accumulative and narrativised, based on our ability to join the dots between different experiences we have undergone, different people we have known. Our personal history is our account of these actions in time. When we lose our memory, we lose our sense of time. We are forced to live without that most constitutive element of our existence – our sense of duration, our succession. Without time, there can be no plot. As Denise Riley writes, 'A life of no time can't be recounted. Your very condition militates against narrative.'

The effect of this is something like a loss of significance. An action or an event, severed from the history that led to it, is void and without consequence. It leads to nothing. 'The whole notion of directedness has gone,' Riley says. The event floats without any weight. It doesn't mean anything, either as an inflection of past events or an indicator of events to follow.

To be informed of an action of our own that we have forgotten is to be forced to take up a position in relation to that action; not ownership, in the usual way of saying *I did that*, but in something more like moral judgement: *I wouldn't do that, I can't believe I did that*. The subjective experience is drained away, and the brutish objectivity of a fact in isolation is all that remains. Motivation is irrelevant. The Alzheimer's patient cannot say where they were; steps cannot be retraced. They take on the air of a convict. They have no alibi.

—

As soon as we are ill, John Berger says, we fear that our illness is unique. Undefined, illimitable, the newly arrived sickness is a threat to our very being. It 'shares in our own uniqueness', he says. This is particularly true of Alzheimer's, which attacks and undermines our very being – our sense of who we are and what we're doing in the world. Every case of Alzheimer's is experienced as completely unique because it is a disease that operates on the bedrock of our uniqueness.

Patients, Berger notes, are typically quite relieved when their illness is named. Whether the name means anything to them is unimportant; it is the name that allows them to have their complaint recognised – they're not making this up, this is a real thing; this is how it works and this is how other people have dealt with it. Armed with a diagnosis, the patient is protected from the ambiguity of their disease. The disease is with them, but not of them. It is depersonalised.

Alzheimer's is not so easily cordoned off. Because it is still incurable, because it is so terribly unique, naming the disease does little to strengthen the patient's position against it. It serves only to confirm their uniqueness, and to make explicit the distinction that from now on will separate them from everyone else. Worse again, their uniqueness is an erasure. Alzheimer's is not an acquisition, like a typical illness – it is not a cancer, or an infection – but a loss barely visible on the surface of the body, a wound that seems to grow from the inside out. A loss that cannot be repaired, only observed, and that has at its end a total blank nothingness.

The naming of Alzheimer's disease is not a positive defence against its effects; it is a wall behind which the struggle of the self to be recognised as more than its disease must take place. The frustration and bitterness of this struggle for recognition is unbearable, because the struggle itself is, in some sense, the disease. The pain is rooted in our diminishing sense of ourselves and our place in the world, a sense that we are being erased. 'All frustration magnifies its own dissimilarity,' Berger says, 'and so nourishes itself.' The Alzheimer's patient is unique in the erasure of their own uniqueness; a vicious feedback loop of frustration, a great dialectical joke.

—

Christmas Day – his last. The family, some cousins included, are gathered in my grandparents' kitchen around mid-morning, as we have been every other year of my life. This is when the children – and I am a child on that day – give Nana and John Joe their Christmas presents. The gifts themselves are inconsequential; it's the ceremony that's important. This year was different because I don't think we got him anything. There would have been no point; it had been a long time since he'd recognised any of his grandchildren, and he would have immediately forgotten any gift we gave him. He could remember Nana, my father, and usually my father's sister. His world had shrunk to those three people, and that kitchen, which he left only to sleep.

Nana always makes an oversized fuss about the small gifts she receives. She paws at the wrapping paper, not wanting to tear it. Once she has been cajoled into action and torn open the package, she will hold the soft lining of a new dressing gown against her face, or bend close to savour the aroma of yet another scented candle. She will beam with happiness, and the sincerity of her appreciation only deepens our sense of embarrassment at having chosen such pedestrian presents. It doesn't matter: she has been brought almost to tears by a jumbo book of wordsearch puzzles. Strangely, when my father and his siblings were young, it was John Joe who would buy their Christmas presents.

When we had finished with the gift-giving that year, we sat around the kitchen chatting. John Joe was quiet in the corner by the fire, smiling sometimes, but mostly unengaged; a little worried and withdrawn, possibly over-whelmed. Someone would occasionally try to tell him what was going on but by then he could barely speak, much less take part in a conversation. If he responded at all, it was usually with one of the stock phrases he would use to deflect questions and gloss over his inability to contribute.

I remember we were about to leave. Everyone was standing up. Clean midwinter light poured through the window at the front of the house; the fire was low in the range. Nana was probably getting anxious about starting to prepare their simple Christmas dinner. We fetched our coats, and began to say our goodbyes. John Joe was holding my mother's hand, I think, when he asked her who she was.

She told him her name. She said she was married to my father.

God help you, he replied.

I am serious when I say the laughter lasted for a minute solid. I looked at my brothers and my cousins scattered around the kitchen and they were bent double, crying laughing. My father was laughing, as much in disbelief as anything – he was being mocked by his demented 82-year old father. Nana didn't know where to look. It was an incredible moment of pure comedic instinct, sharper and sweeter for having come from the very depths of his soul. And it was his soul the line displayed – that warm, joking soul, with a little edge in every dig; piercing, mordant, kind, sincere. It was totally unexpected, and it floored us all.

This was the last moment when I thought to myself, *Yes, that's him*. It was the last time I recognised him as himself and not his disease.

—

A person with dementia will typically become isolated from the existing structures and communities of their lives. They will no longer be able to engage with them. Having lost the capacity to blend in with a crowd, they are set in relief against their traditional environments. To this extent, the disease individualises them, it marks them out. They become, in some sense, more specific; a figure in need of special attention and consideration. They become someone to whom everything must be explained, around whom events must be planned. Their presence, their equanimity, their ability to cope – none of this can be taken for granted any longer. Extra efforts must be made in order for them to follow whatever is happening around them, and in this way they shape what is happening. They may become the most visible and most powerful person in a room, or in one's thoughts. The world may very well begin to revolve around them.

But dementia also dis-individualises people; it destroys the memories, the gestures, the knots that, in the practice of daily life, constitute their sense of themselves and the senses others have of them. Their ability to access the experiences and actions that distinguish them as individuals is gradually erased. They become a person losing by degrees what others would once have recognised as their personality or their character. They sit in the corner of the room, untethered from the people and the conversations happening around them. They can no longer respond in a way that others recognise as emotionally suitable. The usual process of reciprocation is interrupted, becoming jagged and painful. They may begin to opt out of conversations, choosing wilful disconnection over the increasing likelihood of embarrassment or confusion. The world may very well begin to pass them by.

I guess this is something like a dialectic of dementia. A person with dementia becomes an ever-expanding absence that must be cared for, monitored, attended to; a lengthening silence that must be listened to. They become a person disappearing before eyes more conscious and watchful than ever before. We act as if the effort of observation might slow the fade – as if we were watching the sun go down, or waiting for a kettle to boil. The familiar, distinguishing features of a person in this condition become, for us on the outside, signs that the observation is effective. We recognise a tone of voice, a light in the eyes; we say, *That's him*. Even if every day is constructed around the presence of this disappearing person, we celebrate any moment in which we can recognise the person as they were, when we could love them truly without thought of their finitude, without the abscesses that have hollowed out our relationship with them. When they were not set against the sad ongoingness of our lives. When we marked them as special, not different.

—

Judith Butler, in *Giving An Account of Oneself*, writes about the violence of an idea or an ethos that ignores the existing social conditions in which it appears. 'It insists itself into the present as an anachronism,' she says. Despite the antipathy or resistance of those who are forced to live with it, this kind of force refuses to disappear, to fade into the past. It makes a violent claim for its continuing universality, for its ongoing collectivity. It denies the realities of the people on whom it acts, and seeks to replace those realities with one of its own making. 'It not only imposes itself upon the present,' Butler says, 'but also seeks to eclipse the present – and this is precisely one of its violent effects.'

The violence of Alzheimer's is that it substitutes its reality for our own. The experience of the disease is predictable and persistent enough to be transcendent; its violence is a universal violence, which takes no account of the individual suffering under its weight. The particularity of the patient is swallowed up by the collectivity of the diseased, the universality of oblivion. The violence of the disease is not only in how it destroys the patient's perception of their past, but in how it imposes itself on their present. It seeks to define, to overwhelm.

For Butler, a violent universality is that of which no living appropriation can be made. You can't do anything with it, make anything of it. One is simply subject to it. It is, she says, *a deathly thing*. There is no hope of acknowledgement, no reciprocation – it is one-way traffic. A disease like Alzheimer's, a disease of just such violent universality, is set in stone – unbending, dispassionate – and quickly weighs like one too. Butler could easily have been talking about dementia when she described a 'suffering imposed from an indifferent outside at the expense of freedom and particularity'. But I guess it only appears that way: dementia isn't imposed from an indifferent outside, it comes from within.

—

Self-formation is like storytelling: it is a process of delimitation. The storyteller takes responsibility for what happens in the story; they concern themselves with the words on the page. We do the same when we think of ourselves. We block off a part of the world – our body, our mind – and say, this is what I'm responsible for, this is the object I'll work on and refine. 'This work on the self, this act of delimiting,' Butler says, 'takes place within the context of a set of norms that precede and exceed the subject.'

Our single site of responsibility interacts with others, and it develops meaning and consequences outside itself. Really it can never be understood in isolation. The process of accounting for ourselves is shaped by outside forces, even initiated by them. 'I begin my story of myself only in the face of a "you" who asks me to give an account,' says Butler.

But an Alzheimer's patient, almost by definition, loses their self-narrating ability. Their ongoing formation of themselves is impeded by their inability to be recognised, impacted, and changed by other people in the world. In never being transformed by what is outside of them, that which corresponds and inquires, the patient is stopped from growing and becoming positively other than what they were. Their experience is entirely one of decay and stasis, which are two sides of the same time-weathered coin.

—

'The question of ethics,' Butler writes, 'emerges precisely at the limits of our schemes of intelligibility, the site where we ask ourselves what it might mean to continue in a dialogue where no common ground can be assumed.'

Lacking a cure, Alzheimer's can only be mitigated. The primary method is recognition. Beyond physical necessities, the task of the carer is to limit, as best they can, the patient's spiralling disintegration into unrecognisable uniqueness. This is an ethical demand, and it is not simple to meet. As the usual bonds of recognition and connection are broken – as memories fall away, as activities become impossible, as conversation is reduced to silence – there remains the burden and duty of saying: *I see you.* Against the creeping tide of the disease, we are asked to find the previously invisible, unacknowledged commonalities, the slivers of life and being which, too faint and unimportant for everyday notice, nonetheless persist after the louder noises of living have faded away. As if, sitting by the fire with a friend in the evening of his life, we should strain to hear the waves on the distant shore – present all along, underneath the busy hum of the everyday, but only now emerging through the murky quiet.

What Judith Butler said: *Reason's limit is the sign of our humanity.*

see ye in church

John Joe made it through the winter but with the coming of spring his condition worsened and in no time at all we were sitting in the kitchen below just waiting for him to die. Waiting for someone to die is a little like waiting for news, except that you already know what the news is going to be. What you don't know is when it's going to arrive. In the interim, time becomes distorted. It seems to become thinner, because the event on which the time depends has not yet occurred, and also fuller, more meaningful – everything that does happen is notable and is remarked upon. As it is when you find yourself in a very quiet place, every disturbance of the air is subject to a great deal of attention. Everyone is very raw, and everything stands out.

I wrote Niamh a late-night email during this time where I told her that she could learn everything there was to know about my family in twenty-four of those peculiar hours. I told her how tired everyone was, how it seemed like everyone was working so hard just to keep things together. I told her I missed Buddy, our King Charles who had died two months before, and wondered how our two cats were coping with the loss of their canine friend. We were all unusually exposed during this curious endgame and yet there was a tremendous sense of focus that over-took the house when John Joe was decisively confined to the bed and visitors began to arrive not to see how he was, but to say goodbye.

The people who came would sit with Nana for some time, and then quietly make their way up to John Joe's room. After a minute or two, Nana might follow them up. I could often hear their low, gentle voices from the kitchen, sometimes making out the kind words that passed between them, or the silence as Nana began to cry, one hand grip-ping the visitor's hand, the other covering her mouth. They would come back down together and the guest would sit another little while before leaving again. We maintained a steady pool of family in the kitchen, and it felt like we were there to provide a buffer between the ordinary life people were coming from, and the cheerless quiet of John Joe's room. News from one visitor would be told to the next three, and a body of chat grew up through tight loops of repetition. Within a day or two I could recount these stories as if I'd been a part of their creation. I have forgotten them all now, bar one, which I remember only imperfectly.

It was late in the afternoon when Eoin, Nana's brother-in-law, arrived in the kitchen. I was there with Nana, and it was just the three of us. Eoin was a round, gregarious man of about eighty, and he had the cure for shingles. He cured Nana of an awful case just a few years ago, coming three times to the house for a ritual with fire and water, but the talent may have ended with him. Last I heard, none of his children would take it off him. Eoin sat on the couch beneath the window, and the light began to fade while he talked with Nana. I sat at the table across the room, from where the golden evening sun illuminated the top of Eoin's head, but left his face in shadow. The glow from the fire was weak but warm. Eoin had a capacious memory, a fact that would have been almost cruel in that kitchen had he not been a natural storyteller. He'd met a lot of people in his life, doing all sorts of jobs and showing up at all sorts of events, and he retained in his mind an incredibly detailed ledger of their histories, relationships and family connections. Eoin was the kind of man who knew the third cousin of your uncle's second wife's first husband, and he had a story about everyone.

Eoin told us about a woman he met, quite by accident, in a nursing home. He had gone to visit another friend, who happened to be sitting with this woman when he arrived. This lady was very old, very frail, and didn't speak much. Eoin being Eoin, he quickly discovered who she was, where she had grown up, and who her family were. He then produced a piece of information that I still cannot quite believe to be true. Sixty years ago, as a young man, he had gone to a dance in some parish hall near Tullamore. There he watched a small young woman playing an accordion that was almost too big for her to hold. Eoin didn't speak to her on the night, and he had never seen her again, but he was sure the very same woman was now sitting in front of him in the nursing home. He told her that he recognised her and remembered that night in the hall, and she began to weep. It was all so long ago.

—

I stayed for four days while nothing happened. The weather was horrible and everyone was on edge. Everyone knew there were arrangements to be made, a million little things that needed seeing to, but no one wanted to jump the gun. The morbid details of funerals and wakes had to be discussed, but only hesitantly, and never in their house. He wasn't dead yet, after all. He wasn't getting better, but he didn't seem to be getting worse either. There was no way of knowing how long this would go on for.

I had to leave on Wednesday night. I was due to interview some people the following day, and I had to be in Dublin to do it. Part of me wanted to leave: I was very tired, and I wanted to be with Niamh and our cat. I wanted to spend some time in my own life. I packed my bags that evening and went to stay a while in the kitchen below. My cousin was going to give me a lift to the station. Shortly before he arrived, I went up to see John Joe. It was dark outside, and the room was not warm. I stood next to him without saying anything. I had nothing to say. I doubt anything even crossed my mind. I felt utterly blank in John Joe's presence then, as if the kind of silence that often sat between us when he was more fully alive was now complete and universal. I touched his hand, or maybe his shoulder, I can't remember. I could no longer hear the voices in the kitchen. I didn't stay long in that quiet before returning to my seat by the fire. When I sat down again I was hit by an undeniable certainty that I would never see John Joe alive again and I began, slowly at first and then with abandon, to cry my eyes out.

—

I regret that I was not there when the night nurse called to say he would soon be gone. I regret not walking through the garden in the dark, not walking towards the solitary light of my grandmother's kitchen. I regret not hearing the boots stepping onto the frosted gravel in the yard. I regret not seeing Nana's face that night. I regret that I was not there in the bedroom with my family when he breathed his last. I regret leaving for something as silly as work. I regret getting in the car. I regret buying the train ticket at the station. I regret every decision I made the night I left and I regret every decision I made the following day because I was not there when John Joe died. I regret not knowing then how much I wanted to be there. I regret thinking that it didn't matter one way or the other, because I was lying to myself and I don't know why. I regret my weakness. I regret not understanding. I regret that all these decisions were final and that I will never be able to change them. I regret that I will have to live with them always. These are my only regrets.

—

My mother phoned at seven in the morning. When I heard the phone ring I knew what was coming. I slipped out of bed and answered in the hall. I can't remember a single word that was said. I walked around the living room for a few minutes in the dark, checked train times, started packing a bag. Niamh and I lived in an L-shaped, two-room basement flat at the time, on a quiet road just south of the canal. The flat had two windows, one facing north, the other west, and they both looked out onto a fenced-off gravel path. You couldn't see much. It was an arrangement that sometimes made it difficult to know what the weather was like outside and so when I left the flat, I was totally unprepared for the snow that greeted me. I still cannot believe that it snowed that morning, the only morning of the year it did.

I hadn't thought too much about how I would get to the station in time for the next train, assuming I could get a taxi or some sort of bus. But it was Friday morning, and every taxi in Dublin was engaged in bringing people to work in the snow. Traffic was barely moving. I decided it would be quicker to cycle than to get a bus. I walked for fifteen minutes to the nearest public bike station, but there were no bikes. I walked to the next one, five minutes further in the snow, where I found a single bike remaining. I cycled the two and a half miles to the station in the freezing fog of the morning rush hour. I could barely see ahead of me, and buses flew past aggressively as I pedalled down the long stretch of the quays. I hadn't eaten, my bag was heavy, and my legs could barely pedal. The wind was strong and in my face the entire way, at times slowing me until I almost stopped completely.

I arrived at the station, sweating from the cycle and half frozen from the snow – my hair dripping, my jumper soaked through – only to discover I had missed the train by a matter of seconds. I called my mother and told her the whole sorry story. I apologised for missing the train, as if it mattered. I had done everything I could, I said. I was frantic, tired, starving. I didn't know what was going on. My mother told me to go eat something.

—

Nana's kitchen is the kind of room that can feel too full with five people in it, and yet be pleasantly intimate with twelve or fifteen. Still, it was not the place for an event like a wake. More than the brute fact of its size, it would simply be too much strain on Nana to have several hundred people pass through her home over the next few days. Neither she nor the house were up to that, so we decided to have the wake in our house next door. My parents could take most of the pressure off Nana, and she would have a place to go if she needed to get away from everything. This is why, when I got home, John Joe was lying in his coffin in our sitting room.

He was surrounded in the coffin by folds of white satin, dressed in a white shirt, black tie and pressed black trousers. The fine white strands of his hair were carefully brushed and the pallor of his skin warmed with subtle make-up. Thinking of this now I find it hard to believe how little time passed between his death and his arrival in the coffin. It was just a matter of hours. Everyone said he looked so well. Even Nana, when she first saw him there in the coffin, said through tears that he was such a handsome man. She touched his chest and then his head. *Oh, I'd take you to the Gap*, she said, thinking of their first dances together.

On the surface of things, a wake in the countryside is really just a murderously intense period of busywork. They must have been designed to occupy the minds and bodies of the bereaved from the moment of death through to the funeral itself. They also provide an agreed framework for the contributions of neighbours, friends and visitors. There are people, some of our neighbours among them, who are at their very best during a wake. They understand exactly what is required in the situation. They procure industrial-sized boilers for making tea and coffee; locate a dozen extra chairs at half-an-hour's notice; direct troops of unoccupied children in myriad minor tasks. They are direct, efficient, and incredibly helpful. I have never been at a wake without at least one of these people, and I sometimes wonder what kind of disasters would unfold in their absence.

On the Saturday afternoon, we set up a small marquee outside the front door of our house, and I spent most of the evening there with my brothers, my cousins, and Niamh, who had arrived that morning. Hundreds of people came through the door, and we greeted them as they arrived. I met folks I hadn't seen in the guts of ten years: the parents of old school friends, lads I'd played underage football with, distant relatives, people from the other end of the parish. I had known there would be a crowd, but still the reality was overwhelming. Because we were stationed outside the house, we saw people only briefly as they arrived and we had plenty of time to talk about them after they went inside. We laughed every time they assumed Niamh was one of the family, or that my cousin – who is six foot two, red-headed, and looks nothing like the rest of us – was not. We would solemnly shake hands with trains of old men and women offering their condolences and then look to each other and ask, *Who the hell was that?*

It was incredible to me how far some of them had travelled. My aunt's husband showed up on the afternoon of the wake, having flown overnight from Chicago without telling anyone he was coming. The uncle of my uncle's soon-to-be-second-wife drove a distance of fifty miles to shake some hands, drink a cup of tea, and leave again. He knew no one in the family, and had never met John Joe, but he still felt a duty to come. He was a butcher and he gave us a large roasted ham, which was later turned into the best sandwiches we had all weekend.

Niamh went to bed early, worn out from meeting so many people that day, and I found myself in the sitting room with half a dozen men. My father was there, and two of my uncles. Enda, our neighbour from up the road, was telling us stories about all the people of John Joe's time who were now gone. Enda is a soft-faced farmer and lorry-driver in his forties, younger than my father and his brothers. For one reason or another – his father died young, he never left the area, he married late – he spent more time in the homes of an older generation, picking up their stories and their mannerisms, watching their decline close-up.

He went through a familiar litany of names – Gorman, Cahill, Devery, Molloy and Maleney – from a time when this corner of the parish was a busy, well-populated, and deeply social place. To me, these people were barely remembered faces from childhood evenings: the smell of Johnny Gorman's pipe as he sat crumpled in a chair by the fire below; the wide smile of Kieran Molloy in the back room of Cahill's pub, his long narrow legs stretched out in front of him; the laughter of Timmy Devery as he watched us scramble for the sweets and coins he was scattering across the floor of Nana's kitchen some Halloween night long ago. For Enda, and more painfully for Nana, these were vital characters in a story that will soon no longer be told about this place. They were people whose whole lives were here, centred on this community in a way that is maybe not even possible any more.

A wake like John Joe's is not just an opportunity to remember these people and their stories, but also a chance to share and build on those memories, to pass them on and to bind them closer to the people who are living out their own stories in the same place. Both in the people who show up, and in the stories that are told, a wake is a moment when the pattern of a person's life becomes apparent. You see the evidence of a life intertwined and knotted up with other lives, and feel the power of those lines coming together for a final time before someone they all hold in common must be left behind. All that is left of that common thread in the aftermath is the shape of the place they built for themselves to live, and the stories people will in the coming years tell of them.

Listening to Enda that night, I felt nostalgic for a life I have never experienced, and a form of community I will almost certainly never know. John Joe's standing in his community – the community with whom I'd spent the whole day shaking hands – had nothing to do with wealth or success or talent or power. Every story Enda told of John Joe that evening just emphasised how hard he worked to scrape a living out of boggy, stone-filled fields, how he could always be relied upon to help when someone wanted to borrow a machine or needed a hand getting an animal out of a drain, how he was a constant presence on the roads and in the farmyards of every house around. It really wasn't much more than ordinary decency, but it didn't need to be. That sort of kindness goes a long way in a place as familiar and tight-knit as this, where reputations of any kind are not easily shaken off.

I don't need to be told about the limitations of this kind of life. There can be a suffocating intimacy in a world this constrained. Typically shorn of intellectual or cultural variety, there can be cruel borders surrounding what is normal or acceptable. Nonetheless, in the weeks and months after the wake I became convinced that it was this life I wanted for myself. I flicked the switch on a harsh light and looked gravely at the trajectory of my own life. I was disgusted at the idea of never having a home to call my own, dismayed by the way my actions were so determined by my ideas about my career and my desperate grasping for a kind of public – or, to be honest, middle-class – life. Wanting only what I did not possess, I found myself sincerely covetous of John Joe's existence. I would have happily exchanged whatever I knew and thought about the world beyond this place for a sliver of what he had here. I saw the depth of his life reflected in the people who came through the house that evening, the incremental patterning of eighty-three years spent in one place growing richer with every arrival. I wanted to be a part of a community rather than a network. I wanted to take root and echo out. I wanted, more than anything, to create for myself a place where I and everybody I loved would be constant and safe.

For a time, I was like Michael Harding in *Silence*, assured of the wisdom of staying still for the rest of my days. *If I could stay in the house of my mother, the house I was born in, that is a door into the greatest wisdom, the greatest infinity possible,* Harding says. *I'm not going to find out anything more somewhere else.* But I am more like Eoghan than Michael. I know that if you leave, you cannot return. And this departure is not just physical or geographic – if you try to go back, you will find that nothing is the same. The road vanishes as you walk it.

—

Someone told this story at the wake: John Joe goes to sit with an old friend of his in the days before her death. He has known this woman his whole life. Her home is a small cottage at a crossroads and she is in the bedroom in the back of the house. The curtains are drawn, though it is not late, and only one of the woman's daughters is in the house with her. She shows John Joe through to the bedroom and then returns to the kitchen, where she is washing cups and glancing at a muted television in the corner. John Joe sits with the woman in the bedroom. Her memory is in ribbons and she has sunk down into herself. Her eyes flicker when John Joe sits on the stool by the bed but there is no sense of recognition. Her hands twitch at the light cream blanket that covers her. She is very thin now. Her skin is stretched across her cheekbones; her neck is slender and vulnerable. Her mouth hangs open a little and she sometimes makes sounds that could almost be words. Her breathing is slow. Her hair, once black, is now white and shows signs of recent brushing by her daughter. She had always been careful about her appearance. On the table next to the bed is a sealed plastic cup of water with a pink straw shooting out the top, a small golden lamp with a furry shade, and a set of wooden rosary beads.

Sitting by the bed, John Joe is not sure how to start. This is not the first time he's been in a room like this, and he doubts it will be the last. He starts to talk as if they were sitting around the fire in his own kitchen. He reminisces. He talks to her of the days when they were young. When time was slower, and the sunlight so much clearer. He takes her hand. He talks to her of their old friends and the people they used to know. He talks about how she and her friends used to gather on bicycles and fly down the winding roads between here and the town. There were so few cars then, they had the run of the place. He remembers how he would watch them go by from the head of his own road. He had a name for them, her friends and her, and he tells her now that name again. I can't remember the name. It remains a secret between the two of them.

—

Before the hearse left our house for the church on the morning of the funeral, it drove the coffin down to Nana and John Joe's house. I hadn't been expecting this at all. We walked behind in a slow black march as the car made its careful way down the road and then down the hill into the yard. It circled the house once and then headed back out. Walking behind the car as it passed the back door of their house, I felt as sad and as proud as I would feel at any time over the course of the funeral. I can't say why exactly. I could only think of the massive human effort of building a place to live. Of how everything I could see around me had literally been touched and shaped by his hands over such a long period of time. And how it was not enough time, how it could never be enough time, how you would always want more time. I thought of everything his effort had made possible, and how it could all have been other-wise, and how I was so glad it was not. I thought finally that there was no tragedy in this. My grandfather died a happy man – *as happy as a man with two mothers*, as he'd say himself.

—

It fell to my father to deliver the eulogy and he asked me to write it for him. I wrote it in the sitting room on the morning of the funeral. I sat in one corner; John Joe lay in his coffin in the other. The curtains were closed and I wrote in the dark for about an hour. I would be lying if I said I hadn't been thinking, even hoping, that I would be the one who got to write the eulogy. It sounds terrible but I knew I could do a good job. I had even been semi-consciously collecting quotes and ideas I thought could work in a eulogy, though in the end I threw them all out. It turns out that a eulogy is no place for ideas, and it is no place for other people's words.

My aunt read the eulogy aloud at our kitchen table in a teary-eyed preview for the family. My father read it out in the church. Both times it felt like a performance, as if I'd written a score and now the musicians were playing it for an audience. Listening to my father read in the church, I was critical of what I'd written, thinking of ways it could be better and what a second draft would look like. Such dire coldness of habit. Reading it again now, I can hear more of my voice than my father's. The situation demanded a certain text of a certain length on a certain topic, and I believe it met those formal constraints without sounding too much like an exercise in ventrilo-quism. The most beautiful parts are John Joe's own words, which speak most clearly of who he was. Like so much that happens around death, the eulogy is less about the person delivering it than it is about telling a story people want to hear. You have to hit the right notes, thank the right people, finish with a flourish. John Joe knew how to tell a story better than I ever will. I knew that if I could let him speak for himself, as much as possible, he would tell everyone what they needed to hear.

It was easier than I expected to put those words in my father's mouth. There was some comfort in the distance of writing that way – doubly removed: quoting one person for yet another to speak – something so much easier than speaking for myself. I had found it impossible to say anything meaningful that week, or even to do anything useful. I had to be driven around by brothers and cousins, all younger than I was. I was like a child. Writing the eulogy was probably the only occasion during that time when I felt truly connected to what was happening – no longer a mute observer, or even an extra pair of hands, but someone who could contribute in a way that others could not.

Though not typically conscious of it, I have always tried with writing to articulate what those close to me were unable to say. I don't believe that they cannot think these unsaid things, but we are not a dramatic or expressive family at the best of times, and I have long had the sense that it would be my job to preserve some of what they were leaving implicit, to give it a different kind of presence in the world. Looking back, I see the evidence of this even in teenage notebooks, when I wanted to scream about how stifling, how sad, how hopeless I felt this place could be. Almost every decent word I've written in my life has come out of this impulse to make explicit what would otherwise be hidden, overlooked, soon lost.

I believe this also to be the root of whatever sadness I carry with me in life. I feel a terrible need to go beyond the places my family can go – to parse and interpret what they think, say and do; to locate their actions in a context that, for reasons more economic than personal, they cannot easily access. They have given me the tools to separate myself from them, to see them in a way in which they cannot see themselves. It is rare that these tools have made us feel closer. The eulogy may well be the only time when it has happened, and then it was because I was speaking as someone else. I had to forget myself, remove myself from the picture, say simply what needed to be said.

More often, it feels as if I'm living somewhere apart from them, watching them, in some subtle but definitive way, cut off from the true reality of their world. By observing and interpreting that world, and most of all by writing about it, I deny myself the possibility of really living in it. It falls away from me and I'm left only with what is on the page. I take what flows between people who have a common language and I pull it out, make something else out of it. I am not unaware of the violence latent in this act, or the damage it can do on all sides. I'm often afraid that I'm using my family more than I let myself believe. The versions of them that exist in these words are really little more than figments of my imagination. The fear is that I would come to value them more as characters in my story than as people in their own right, that I would leave them exposed, that I would bring them to a place where they would not recognise themselves.

I can listen to them as much as I like, with as much intent and concentration as I can muster, but I cannot tell their stories the way that John Joe would have told them, or the way that people like Enda and Eoin could tell them. I find myself speaking from a different place, and to a different set of ears. I'm not sure I could change this, even if I wanted to. I might desire to live what I mistakenly imagine to be the simple life of my grandfather, but I cannot. I have arrived too late. I'm wearing the wrong clothes, I would look a fool. The way back to that imagined life is closed, and none of these words are ever going to teach me how to follow in the footsteps of the dead. I have to remember what I can, and write it down. The further I have gone into this job of writing about one family in one place – the family I was born into, the place where I grew up – the greater the distance has grown between me and all of that. Perhaps from the beginning it was unbridgeable. What a melancholy act. There is no redemption in it.

—

The old parish priest, who had recently left the area, returned to say the mass. It was a kindness John Joe would have appreciated. I remember him saying that when you mentioned the name John Joe, everyone around here knew who you meant. You didn't have to specify: there was only one John Joe. He didn't talk about how, for years, the one-and-only John Joe could be heard talking during mass with his friends in the back pew. But he was probably thinking about it.

In the church they played 'The Rocks of Bawn' during communion, and 'Wild Mountain Thyme' as the coffin was wheeled out. My father and his brothers carried it down the steps from the church door and slid it into the hearse waiting at the gate. I remember us looking at the coffin through the glass and the welling up of a momentary sadness. My youngest brother began to cry and I pulled his head to my shoulder without thinking. It's probably the only time I've ever hugged him – this is what I mean when I say we're not a dramatic or expressive family.

I was one of six brothers and cousins who carried the coffin from the hearse through the gates of the cemetery. A team of men – neighbours and friends – had been digging down there all morning and the dirt was heaped beside the newly opened grave. On the other side of the hole someone had lined up the flowers. We laid the coffin down on thick, pale planks by the waiting earth.

The names of John Joe's father and mother were carved on a stone beside the new grave. His father had also died at the age of eighty-two. A more distant ancestor, dead a century before John Joe was born, lay a hundred yards away in the ground of the old monastery. Many of the men who dug the grave – farmers with thick hands and mud-stained boots – will end their days there, as will my own father. Maybe I will too, though I'm inclined towards cremation myself. Still, it wouldn't be a bad spot to spend eternity. From the little incline where our plot resides, you can look over the rows of gravestones to the river, which comes right up to the cemetery wall when in flood. You can hear the beat of the swans' wings as they come low across the water. A tall crowd of fir trees have grown up around the place and their fallen needles quieten footsteps on the paths.

The graveside ceremony was short and not just because it was beginning to rain. The priest said a few words, and we had another decade of the rosary. When enough had been said, my father and his brothers took hold of the ropes that lay under the coffin. They strained the lining of their suits as they lowered it quietly into the ground. We took Nana to the car when they began to shovel the dirt back into the grave. She could never bear the sound of stone and earth falling thoughtlessly on coffinwood.